AF222100

The Lyrics Of The
Original Records

Compiled and edited by
Heinz Gerstenmeyer

Bibliographische Information der Deutschen Nationalbibliothek
Die Deutsche Nationalbibliothek verzeichnet diese Publikation in
der Deutschen Nationalbibliographie; detaillierte bibliographische
Daten sind im Internet über *http://dnb.d-nb.de* abrufbar.

Dedicated to
Danny Sugerman
(1954–2005)

Limited Edition
December 2009

Herstellung und Verlag:
Books on Demand GmbH, Norderstedt

ISBN: 978-3-8391-2911-1

Contents

The Original Songbooks

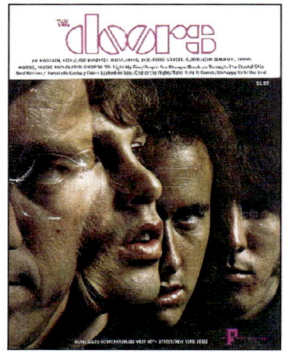

USA, September 1967

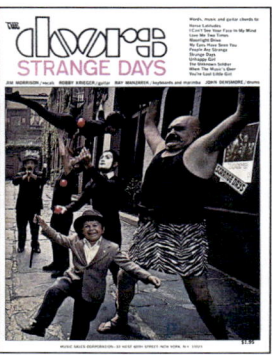

USA, March 1968

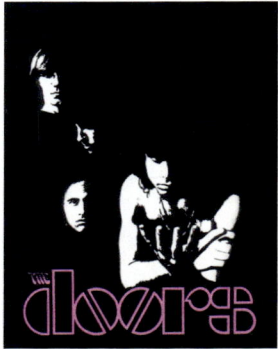

USA, March 1968

USA, December 1968

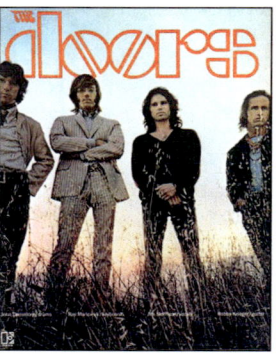

USA, December 1968

USA, March 1970

USA, October 1969
(Front)

USA, October 1969
(Back)

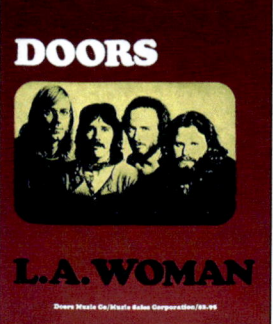

USA, May 1971

Editor's Note

To each album of The Doors a songbook was published which included the lyrics, chords and piano arrangements to every song. Unfortunately none of these books were superintended by The Doors, as Robby Krieger has confirmed to me in April 1989. The lyrics were transcripts of the recorded version, so naturally these books were full of partly gross mistakes. Moreover, the lyrics were adjusted to the piano arrangements, which means that repeated lines, verses, choruses, and all the improvised parts have been left off.

In September 1991 Danny Sugerman released the songbook *The Complete Illustrated Lyrics*. Unfortunately again, he didn't bother about the correctness of the lyrics and mainly followed the words of the original songbooks.

In July 1992 I finally was able to publish my carefully elaborated transcript of The Doors' lyrics, where I had, with the help of a lot of British and American friends, including Robby Krieger, eliminated as well as all mistakes of the original songbooks. But shortly before it was released in Germany, Danny Sugerman stepped in and worked as superintendent between my manuscript and his book. The result was that many mistakes from the original songbooks were put in again, and also some new ones by Danny Sugerman. This version of The Doors' lyrics, which has also been published in November 1992 in the Delta paperback edition of Danny Sugerman's book, is the 'official' version until today. It is also included in all of The Doors' CD-Boxes that have been released since 1999, on all individual CDs that have been released since March 2007, on the official Doors website, and it is generally widely spread in the Internet.

This book contains the lyrics of the 63 studio songs The Doors have released during their active career with Jim Morrison, exactly as they have been sung on the original LPs. Three of the songs are cover versions, which are printed exactly the way Jim Morrison sang them.

I could clarify the doubtful passages by comparison to all available mono, stereo and DVD mixes, alternative studio takes, live versions, and handwritten lyrics by Jim Morrison.

The songs *When The Music's Over*, *Hello I Love You*, *Five To One*, *The Soft Parade* and *Peace Frog* feature vocal tracks where Jim Morrison simultaneously sings different words. I have put these parts in columns and have printed the words of the different, simultaneously sung vocal tracks in one line.

Included are also all available handwritten lyrics by Jim Morrison, facsimiles of the lyric sheets which were enclosed to some of the original records, and 28 contemporary American and British record reviews.

124 pages. Illustrated with 9 color and 27 black and white illustrations.

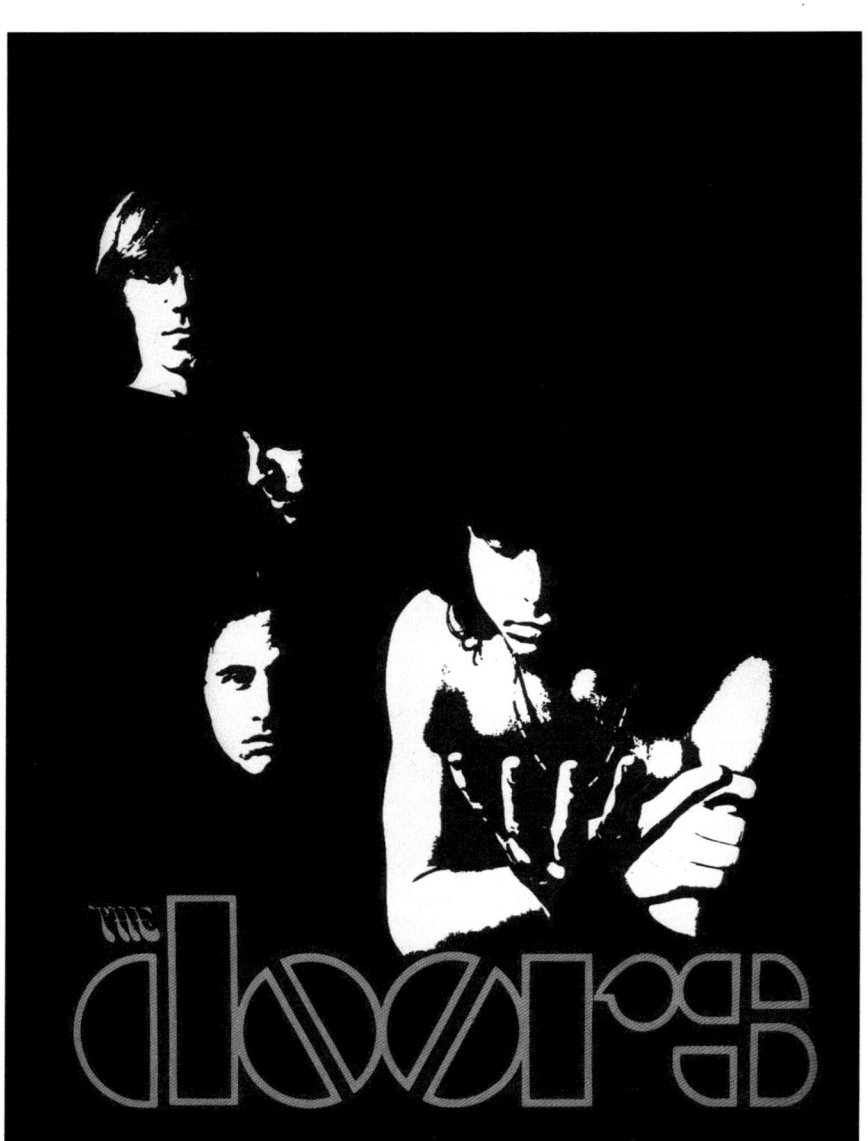

Vibrations, USA, October 1967
The New Lyric Imagination: The Doors

Ever since the beginning of this year, words are coming back. Lyrics are growing as people are finding a new courage to express themselves. This connection between lyricism and honesty is enriching songs, their writers and their listeners.

Much has been said this year and last about eroticism and how being erotic really differs from just having sexual desire. Freud already said this years ago when he cautioned that libido was not to be interpreted as sex drive but as a more basic life drive including sexual energy.

Having cleared this up, we can talk about The Doors' album as music without having to launch into intellectual discussions of how Eros and Pathos lurk behind Ethos in every Doors song. They do.

But the Los Angeles group can't be described by album cover credits or description of their musical arrangements (Freudian rock-blues) and what instruments play when. This is to say that The Doors are not only studio musicians, but live performers as well.

It begins when Jim Morrison in leather-epauletted jacket sears vocals at you and on his good days sends you to the inner rooms of your mind. And you hold his words with your emotions – and your mind gasps at yourself. Jim Morrison's voice does for The Doors' sound what Elvin Bishop's lead guitar does for the Paul Butterfield Band. It raves. But there is much more, for Jim's voice flows with Ray Manzarek's precise organ, which can come in whenever it is needed to enrich the sound. Listen to John Densmore's solid drumming coming through like a heart beat in *Soul Kitchen*. And then Robby Krieger, who plays an economical, tight, precise guitar, lets loose on *Light My Fire* and shows he can play loose, wide-sleeved flowing ragas. Jim's voice then rushes in to finish *Light My Fire* – a voice that here is erotic and immensely able to give each phrase the soul it needs to make one know the song. He puts on a play and what comes out is very naturally psychedelic and open.

Break On Through begins to get you into what The Doors are doing. A rhythm line is laid down, suggesting the melody to come. Anticipation. The secret of all great music and drama. Manzarek does it with the organ in *Break On Through*; Morrison then sings the hidden melody. And the climax comes when the volume goes way up to crescendo, but notes are held, rhythm is held, and the song organically holds together. So do you, listening. For your sanity isn't being attacked.

Soul Kitchen starts the same way. Manzarek on the organ, reinforced by a bass line which Manzarek plays himself live and is double tracked on the album. The first drum beats by John Densmore are already the first three notes of the hidden melody. Then the melody builds up into less of the spoken word and more of raw tempo.

Break On Through, *Soul Kitchen*, *The Crystal Ship* and *Twentieth Century Fox* are like a sonata in four movements. *The Crystal Ship*, which picks up from the slowdown end on *Soul Kitchen*, is the slow movement. *Twentieth Century Fox* is the rondo or lively movement, the fast recapitulation of what has been said. If one understands the three previous songs, one can really come out and tease unerotic 'Twentieth Century Fox'.

Light My Fire is different in intention. It doesn't start the same way as the above songs. It is set up differently, with Morrison this time singing the rhythm line. There is no hidden melody; the instrumental break is beautiful. And with interest in R & B at an all time high, it is no surprise that *Light My Fire* became #1 in the country.

Follow the thought train of their song *The End* in one of its spontaneous live performances at New York's *The Scene*: "I want to tell you about / The world and the wagon wheel / Turning all the time / You got to try harder / I want you to see where I'm at / I want you to know how I feel / With the wagon wheel."

The End. It is really a song about the beginning of what is to come. It begins as a raga and weaves thoughts. While not the most melodic Doors song, it has its power sunk into the words – the words of a trip (or highway) of discovery. A voyage of the outer traveler. Jim does it live with all the vigor of his delivery. And each time the song is sung, he adds words and ideas from recent events to make it more personal to you.

So *The End*, since it is more expression and less communication than many rock heads want, emerges as a specialty song. One that will appeal only to those who believe in the new lyric imagination.

These six songs bring The Doors through to the other side.

Crawdaddy!, USA, May 1967
Rock Is Rock – A Discussion Of A Doors Song

Very few people have the balls to talk about 'rock and roll' anymore. REVOLVER made it difficult. BETWEEN THE BUTTONS, SMILE, and The Doors' LP are making it impossible. 'Pop music' is definable only by pointing at a current chart; The Doors are not 'pop', they are simply 'modern music'. The term applies not because rock has achieved the high standards of mainstream music, but conversely because rock has *absorbed* mainstream music, has become the leader, the arbiter of quality, the music of today. The Doors, Brian Wilson, The Stones *are* modern music, and contemporary 'jazz' and 'classical' composers must try to measure up.

THE DOORS is an album of magnitude. There are no flaws. The birth of the group is in this album, and it's as good as anything in rock. The awesome fact about The Doors is that they will improve. This album is too good to be 'explained' note by note, song by song. That sort of thing could only be boring. Is there really any point in saying something like

"The instrumental in *Light My Fire* builds at the end into a truly visual orgasm in sound" when the reader can at any time put the album onto the phonograph and experience that orgasm himself? Descriptive criticism is obviously a waste of time, where quality is involved. It might be valid to make a comment like: "the 'come' sequence at the end of *Light My Fire* is the most powerfully controlled release of accumulated instrumental kineticism known on record" but in the context of an album as great and as implicational and as able-to-change history as this one, comments like that dissatisfy and bore because they're simply obvious.

Soul Kitchen is nice. It's a nice little song about desire, a routine drama in which Jim points out that it looks like it's time for him to go but he'd "really like to stay here all night". And he does stay, and The Doors do their usual 'boy gets girl' instrumental routine, and then Jim lampoons his own posturing, repeating "The clock says it's time to close now" but then saying "I *know* I've got to go now". "I'd really like to stay here all night" changes from effective plea into bitter irony. Jim obviously didn't give that much of a damn about the girl in this case, so something must have been really bothering him. This leads us to the really stunning revelation that sexual desire is merely the particularization of some more far-reaching dissatisfaction.

The message of *Soul Kitchen* is of course "learn to forget". The actual words "learn to forget" are repeated four times at the end of the second verse, and are never returned to in any way. The success of this song is due to the fact that the playing and the other words of the song are almost totally unrelated to the message, and as a result they serve as emphasis instead of confusion. It's possible to get stoned for days by listening to this song. "Learn to forget" – what power that phrase has! Above all, it's an echo of the Sophoclean section of *The End* (echo because the album is programmed circularly for repeated listening) in which it becomes necessary to kill the father. As Paul Rothchild says, "'Kill the father' means, kill all of those things within yourself that are instilled in you and are not of yourself." Obviously, "learn to forget" could easily have the same meaning to Jim. But *The End*, which is a truly beautiful, perfected, polished intellectual statement, cannot communicate as powerfully as *Soul Kitchen*, since the latter is not on an intellectual level at all. *The End* is great to listen to when you're high (or any other time), but *Soul Kitchen* will get you high.

Break On Through   (Jim Morrison)

You know the day destroys the night
Night divides the day
Try to run, try to hide

Break on through to the other side
Break on through to the other side
Break on through to the other side, *yeah*

We chased our pleasures here
Dug our treasures there
But can you still recall, time we cried

Break on through to the other side
Break on through to the other side

Yeah!
Come on, babe…

Everybody loves my baby
Everybody loves my baby
She gets
She gets
She gets
She gets
Yeah...

I found an island in your arms
Country in your eyes
Arms that chained us, eyes that lied

Break on through to the other side
Break on through to the other side
Break on through – *wow!*
Oh yeah…

Made the scene, week to week
Day to day, hour to hour
Gate is straight, deep and wide

Break on through to the other side
Break on through to the other side

Break on through
Break on through
Break on through
Break on through

Yeah!
Yeah!
Yeah!
Yeah!
Yeah!
Yeah!
Yeah!
Yeah!
Yeah!

Soul Kitchen   (Jim Morrison)

Well, the clock says it's time to close now
I guess I'd better go now
I'd really like to stay here all night

The cars crawl past all stuffed with eyes
Street lights shed their hollow glow
Your brain seems bruised with numb surprise
Still one place to go
Still one place to go

Let me sleep all night in your soul kitchen
Warm my mind near your gentle stove
Turn me out and I'll wander, baby
Stumbling in the neon groves

Well, your fingers weave quick minarets
Speaking secret alphabets
I light another cigarette
Learn to forget
Learn to forget
Learn to forget
Learn to forget

Let me sleep all night in your soul kitchen
Warm my mind near your gentle stove
Turn me out and I'll wander, baby
Stumbling in the neon groves – *yeah...*

Well, the clock says it's time to close now
I know I have to go now
I really wanna stay here all night
All night
All night

The Crystal Ship   (Jim Morrison)

Before you slip into unconsciousness
I'd like to have another kiss
Another flashing chance at bliss
Another kiss, another kiss

The days are bright and filled with pain
Enclose me in your gentle rain
The time you ran was too insane
We'll meet again, we'll meet again

Oh tell me where your freedom lies
The streets are fields that never die
Deliver me from reasons why
You'd rather cry, I'd rather fly

The crystal ship is being filled
A thousand girls, a thousand thrills
A million ways to spend your time
When we get back, I'll drop a line

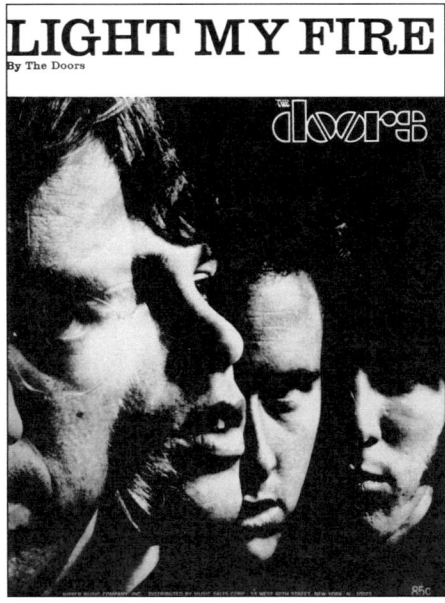

Twentieth Century Fox   (Jim Morrison)

Well, she's fashionably lean
And she's fashionably late, babe
She'll never rank a scene
She'll never break a date

But she's no drag, just watch the way she walks

She's a Twentieth Century Fox
She's a Twentieth Century Fox
No tears, no fears, no ruined years, no clocks
She's a Twentieth Century Fox, oh yeah

She's the queen of cool
And she's the lady who waits
Since her mind left school
It never hesitates

She won't waste time on elementary talk

'Cause she's a Twentieth Century Fox
She's a Twentieth Century Fox
Got the world locked up inside a plastic box

She's a Twentieth Century Fox, oh yeah
Twentieth Century Fox, my babe
Twentieth Century Fox, my...
She's a Twentieth Century Fox

Alabama Song   (Bertold Brecht / Arr.: Jim Morrison)

Oh show me the way to the next whiskey-bar
Oh don't ask why, oh don't ask why
Show me the way to the next whiskey-bar
Oh don't ask why, oh don't ask why
For if we don't find the next whiskey-bar
I tell you we must die, I tell you we must die
I tell you, I tell you, I tell you we must die

Oh moon of Alabama
We now must say good-bye
We've lost our good old mamma
And must have whiskey, oh you know why
Oh moon of Alabama
We now must say good-bye
We've lost our good old mamma
And must have whiskey, oh you know why
Yeah

Oh show me the way to the next little girl
Oh don't ask why, oh don't ask why
Show me the way to the next little girl
Oh don't ask why, oh don't ask why
For if we don't find the next little girl
I tell you we must die, I tell you we must die
I tell you, I tell you, I tell you we must die

Oh moon of Alabama
We now must say good-bye
We've lost our good old mamma
And must have whiskey, oh you know why

Light My Fire   (Robby Krieger & Jim Morrison)

You know that it would be untrue
You know that I would be a liar
If I was to say to you
Girl, we couldn't get much higher

Come on, baby, light my fire
Come on, baby, light my fire
Try to set the night on fire

The time to hesitate is through
No time to wallow in the mire
Try now we can only lose
And our love become a funeral pyre

Come on, baby, light my fire
Come on, baby, light my fire
Try to set the night on fire, *yeah...*

The time to hesitate is through
No time to wallow in the mire
Try now we can only lose
And our love become a funeral pyre

Come on, baby, light my fire
Come on, baby, light my fire
Try to set the night on fire, *yeah!*

You know that it would be untrue
You know that I would be a liar
If I was to say to you
Girl, we couldn't get much higher

Come on, baby, light my fire
Come on, baby, light my fire
Try to set the night on fire
Try to set the night on fire
Try to set the night on fire
Try to set the night on fire

Back Door Man   (Willie Dixon & Chester Burnett / Arr.: Jim Morrison)

Right – yeah! Go ahead! Yeah! Yeah! C'mon! Yeah!
Yeah, come on!

I am a – yeah, I'm a back door man
I'm a back door man
The men don't know, but the little girls understand

Well, all you people that trying to sleep
I'm out there making with my midnight creep – *yeah…*
'Cause I'm a back door man
The men don't know, but the little girls understand
Alright, yeah!

You men eat your dinner, eat your pork and beans
I eat more chicken any man ever seen – *yeah, yeah*
I'm a back door man – *wha!*
The men don't know, but the little girls understand

Well, I'm a back door man
I'm a back door man
Well, baby – I'm a back door man
The men don't know, but the little girls understand

I Looked At You   (Jim Morrison)

I looked at you
You looked at me
I smiled at you
You smiled at me

And we're on our way
No, we can't turn back, babe
Yeah, we're on our way
And we can't turn back
'Cause it's too late, too late,
    too late, too late, too late

And we're on our way
No, we can't turn back, babe
Yeah, we're on our way
And we can't turn back
Yeah, yeah
(All right, come on!
Yeah, all right, babe)

I walked with you
You walked with me
I talked to you
You talked to me

And we're on our way
No, we can't turn back – *yeah!*
Yeah, we're on our way
And we can't turn back – *yeah…*
'Cause it's too late, too late,
    too late, too late, too late

And we're on our way
No, we can't turn back
Yeah, we're on our way
And we can't turn back
'Cause it's too late, too late,
    too late, too late, too late

End Of The Night   (Jim Morrison)

Take the highway to the end of the night
End of the night, end of the night
Take a journey to the bright midnight
End of the night, end of the night

Realms of bliss, realms of light
Some are born to sweet delight
Some are born to sweet delight
Some are born to the endless night

End of the night
End of the night
End of the night
End of the night

Realms of bliss, realms of light
Some are born to sweet delight
Some are born to sweet delight
Some are born to the endless night

End of the night
End of the night
End of the night
End of the night

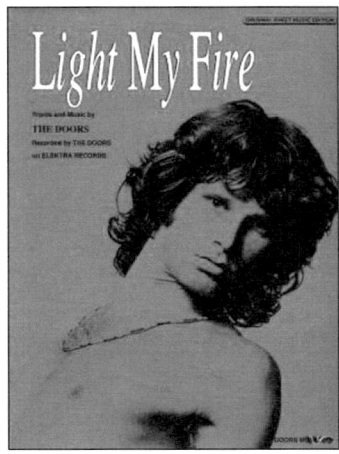

Take It As It Comes   (Jim Morrison)

Time to live, time to lie
Time to laugh, time to die

Take it easy, baby
Take it as it comes
Don't move too fast
When you want your love to last
Ah, you've been moving much too fast

Time to walk, time to run
Time to aim your arrows at the sun

Take it easy, baby
Take it as it comes
Don't move too fast
When you want your love to last
Ah, you've been moving much too fast

Go real slow
You'll like it more and more
Take it as it comes
Specialize in having fun

Take it easy, baby
Take it as it comes
Don't move too fast
When you want your love to last
Ah, you've been
moving much too fast
moving much too fast
moving much too fast

The End   (Jim Morrison)

This is the end, beautiful friend
This is the end, my only friend,
the end

Of our elaborate plans,
the end
Of everything that stands,
the end
No safety or surprise,
the end
I'll never look into your eyes again

Can you picture what will be,
so limitless and free,
desperately in need
of some stranger's hand,
in a desperate land

Lost in a Roman wilderness of pain
And all the children are insane
All the children are insane
Waiting for the summer rain, *yeah...*

There's danger on the edge of town
Ride the king's highway, baby
Weird scenes inside the gold mine
Ride the highway west, baby

Ride the snake
Ride the snake
to the lake,
the ancient lake, baby
The snake is long,
seven miles
Ride the snake
He's old
and his skin is cold

The West is the best
The West is the best
Get here and we'll do the rest

The blue bus is calling us
The blue bus is calling us
Driver, where you taking us?

The killer awoke before dawn
He put his boots on
He took a face from the ancient gallery
And he walked on down the hall

He went into the room where his sister lived, then...
then he... paid a visit to his brother and then he...
he walked on down the hall, *yeah*

And he came to a door
And he looked inside
"Father?"
"Yes, son?"
"I want to kill you.
Mother, I want to..."
Well, all right, yeah! Come on, mom, yeah

Come on, baby, take a chance with us
Come on, baby, take a chance with us
Come on, baby, take a chance with us
and meet me at the back of the
blue bus, doing a
blue rock, on the
blue bus, doing a
blue rock
Come on, *yeah...*

Kill! Kill! Kill! Kill! Kill! Kill! Do it...

This is the end, beautiful friend
This is the end, my only friend,
the end

It hurts to set you free,
but you'll never follow me

The end of laughter and soft lies
The end of nights we tried to die

This is the end

THE doors
STRANGE DAYS

Words, music and guitar chords to:

Horse Latitudes
I Can't See Your Face In My Mind
Love Me Two Times
Moonlight Drive
My Eyes Have Seen You
People Are Strange
Strange Days
Unhappy Girl
The Unknown Soldier
When The Music's Over
You're Lost Little Girl

JIM MORRISON / vocals   ROBBY KRIEGER / guitar   RAY MANZAREK / keyboards and marimba   JOHN DENSMORE / drums

$1.95

MUSIC SALES CORPORATION / 33 WEST 60TH STREET / NEW YORK, N.Y. 10023

Rolling Stone, USA, 23 November 1967
Strange Days

The Doors are an amazing group. Each of them are highly competent and talented musicians; yet music is only secondary to what they are doing. They are violently anti-commercial in their stance and their approach, and yet the finished product is highly commercial. And it would also appear that vocalist Jim Morrison is making a direct appeal to the pubescent market, but upon closer examination, it turns out that he is not.

As musicians, The Doors are very good. Their excellence of musicianship, however, is not seen as individuals, because they do nothing really new or different as soloists. Their excellence is together as a group – the total effect they achieve. The group is original and highly evocative.

Many of the chord progressions and figures are easily recognizable from their first album. Except for the addition of an occasional bass, the instrumentation is nearly identical to the previous LP. Through very logical development, they have improved their original methods and techniques with more effective instrumentation (a variety of keyboard sounds, a lot of slide guitar, and strongly musical electronic bridges). They have not attempted to make any big changes in direction or music (like so many groups mistakenly feel obligated to), but have refined and enriched their previous efforts. Consequently their new album has all the power and energy of the first LP, but is more subtle, more intricate and much more effective.

On a track like *Unhappy Girl*, the various instrumental pieces and the vocal combine perfectly. The effect is overwhelming. *I Can't See Your Face In My Mind* is the only disappointing song on the record; it's mild without justification.

My Eyes Have Seen You, *Strange Days* and *Love Me Two Times* all have the same commercial potential of *Light My Fire*. They are heavy, evocative and climactic pieces.

As was strongly hinted in their first album, The Doors conceive their efforts primarily in terms of drama rather than in terms of music. The music is not meant to be particularly virtuoso or experimental. It is played to be dramatically meaningful.

Beginning with long hair and patterns of dress, rock and roll has become increasingly visual. Rock and roll has become theatre. Jimi Hendrix and The Who seem practically primitive next to The Doors.

Many people don't care to see Jim Morrison making it with his microphone in the manner of Mick Jagger nor do they especially want to watch him writhing on the floor. If they don't, then they suggest he is selling out to commercialism, has an old-fashioned concept of rock and roll or something. However, what's actually taking place on stage, and what Morrison is doing, is about 3000 years old-fashioned and very contemporary in approach.

Music is very sensual and it is particularly obvious in rock and roll. Morrison is just not making any bones about it. He's doing what comes naturally.

One must think of The Doors in a theatrical rather than a musical way. Their whole album, individual songs and especially the final track, are constructed in the five parts of tragedy. Like Greek drama, you know when the music's over because there is catharsis. And, as The Doors suggest in their closing song, "When the music's over," you "turn out the light."

IT, USA, 5–19 January 1968
Strange Doors

"Go through THE DOORS and find STRANGE DAYS." So the latest ad from Elektra exhorts for the American foursome's latest offering. At first it is hard to see what all the fuss is about. There is none of the dynamism of Hendrix, the delicate mysticism of The Beatles, or even the unpredictability of The Stones and a dozen other good groups on the scene.

With the exception of the narrative *Horse Latitudes*, each number is beautifully thought out and somewhat conventionally arranged. Perhaps herein lies much of the record's appeal, it's such a pleasant change. Listen especially to the evocative organ work on the title track, the urgent *Love Me Two Times*, and the beautiful guitar phrases on *People Are Strange*. The curious rather deadpan voice of the singer sets the mood for the whole of this album, a kind of sad and painful truthfulness – this really comes across in the haunting *I Can't See Your Face In My Mind*.

One criticism is that the marathon last track is a bit of a drag, a little too contrived and it doesn't quite come off. But this really is a nice album. Just give it a chance, there are some strange and beautiful things said here. I rate it a whole lot more than their first LP.

High Fidelity Magazine, USA, January 1968
Strange Days

The Doors are generically a psychedelic group, utilizing a cornucopia of often intriguing electronic sonic devices and boasting a healthy degree of musical aplomb. Their sound is unique in its relative freedom from overly distorted hurricanes of acoustical storms; others could learn from them on this count. They draw lightly from blues; only one song, *Love Me Two Times*, is firmly etched in that idiom. Elsewhere they concentrate on producing a sort of undulating harmonic effect. Chords progress less by definite steps than by oozing in and out of focus. Lead vocalist Jim Morrison possesses a voice that is at once rough and soft. Not especially beautiful as voices go, it nonetheless works well within the group's style and helps to contribute to a completely integrated ensemble sound. My only reservation is that though the current album is no less interesting than the first, it isn't much different. The Doors have good basic ideas, but in a field as capricious as rock things happen quickly. They would do well to expand their approach.

Time, USA, 12 January 1968
Strange Days

The Doors have reached that point in fame at which they can now simultaneously have police problems in New Haven, Connecticut, appear in *Vogue*, and be praised for this album.

Some high points: *Moonlight Drive* and *My Eyes Have Seen You* have a rare quality of quiet sensuality, while *Strange Days* and *Unhappy Girl* tell of alienation and aloneness with cool emotion.

Strange Days   (Jim Morrison)

Strange days have found us
Strange days have tracked us down
They're going to destroy
Our casual joys
We shall go on playing or find a new town
Yeah!

Strange eyes fill strange rooms
Voices will signal their tired end
The hostess is grinning
Her guests sleep from sinning
Hear me talk of sin and you know this is it
Yeah!

Strange days have found us
And through their strange hours we linger alone
Bodies confused
Memories misused
As we run from the day to a strange night of stone

You're Lost Little Girl   (Robby Krieger)

You're lost, little girl
You're lost, little girl
You're lost
Tell me who
are you?

Think that you know what to do
Impossible? Yes, but it's true
I think that you know what to do, girl
Sure that you know what to do

You're lost, little girl
You're lost, little girl
You're lost
Tell me who
are you?

Think that you know what to do
Impossible? Yes, but it's true
I think that you know what to do, girl
Sure that you know what to do

You're lost, little girl
You're lost, little girl
You're lost

Love Me Two Times   (Robby Krieger)

Love me two times, baby
Love me twice today
Love me two times, girl
I'm going away
Love me two times, girl
One for tomorrow
One just for today
Love me two times
I'm going away

Love me one time
Could not speak
Love me one time
Yeah, my knees got weak
Love me two times, girl
Last me all through the week
Love me two times
I'm going away
Love me two times
I'm going away
All right, yeah!

Love me one time
Could not speak
Love me one time, baby
Yeah, my knees got weak
Love me two times, girl
Last me all through the week
Love me two times
I'm going away

Love me two times, babe
Love me twice today
Love me two times, babe
'Cause I'm going away
Love me two times, girl
One for tomorrow
One just for today
Love me two times
I'm going away

Love me two times
I'm going away
Love me two times
I'm going away

Unhappy Girl   (Jim Morrison)

Unhappy girl
Left all alone
Playing solitaire
Playing warden to your soul
You are locked
in a prison
of your
own devise

And you can't believe
What it does to me
See you
Crying

Unhappy girl
Tear your web away
Saw through all your bars
Melt your cell today
You are caught
in a prison
of your
own devise

Unhappy girl
Fly fast away
Don't miss your chance
To swim in mystery
You are dying
in a prison
of your
own devise

Unhappy Girl

Unhappy girl,
Left all alone
Playing solitaire
Playing warders to your soul,
you are locked in a prison
of your own / device
And you can't / believe
What / it does/to me,
To see you
Crying

Unhappy girl,
Tear your web away
Saw thru all your / plans
Melt your cell/today
you are caught
in a prison
of your own / device

Unhappy girl,
Fly fast / away
Don't miss your / chance
To swim in
Mystery
You are dying / in a prison
of your own / / device)

Horse Latitudes   (Jim Morrison)

When the still sea conspires an armor
And her sullen and aborted currents
Breed tiny monsters,
True sailing is dead.

Awkward instant
And the first animal is jettisoned,
Legs furiously pumping
Their stiff green gallop,
And heads bob up
Poise
Delicate
Pause
Consent
In mute nostril agony
Carefully refined
And sealed over.

That lap against our side.
Nothing left open, + no Time To decide
river ita handlake.
We've stepped into a river on our
Moonlight drive.

Let's swim To The moon
Let's climb thru The Tide
You reach a hand to hold me
But I can't be your guide
Its easy to love you as I watch you glide
We're falling Thru wet forests on our
Moonlight drive.

Moonlight Drive   (Jim Morrison)

Let's swim to the moon, *uh-huh*
Let's climb through the tide
Penetrate the evening
that the city sleeps to hide
Let's swim out tonight, love
It's our turn to try
Parked beside the ocean on our
Moonlight drive

Let's swim to the moon, *uh-huh*
Let's climb through the tide
Surrender to the waiting worlds
that lap against our side
Nothing left open
and no time to decide
We've stepped into a river on our
Moonlight drive

Let's swim to the moon
Let's climb through the tide
You reach a hand to hold me
But I can't be your guide
Easy *a*-to love you
as I watch you glide
Falling through wet forests on our
Moonlight drive, baby
Moonlight drive

Come on, baby, gonna take a little ride
Going down by the ocean side
Gonna get real close, get real tight
Baby, gonna drown tonight
Going down
Down
Down

People Are Strange   (Jim Morrison)

People are strange
when you're a stranger
Faces look ugly
when you're alone
Women seem wicked
when you're unwanted
Streets are uneven
when you're down

When you're strange
Faces come out of the rain
When you're strange
No one remembers your name
When you're strange
When you're strange
When you're strange

People are strange
when you're a stranger
Faces look ugly
when you're alone
Women seem wicked
when you're unwanted
Streets are uneven
when you're down

When you're strange
Faces come out of the rain
When you're strange
No one remembers your name
When you're strange
When you're strange
When you're strange
All right, yeah

When you're strange
Faces come out of the rain
When you're strange
No one remembers your name
When you're strange
When you're strange
When you're strange

My Eyes Have Seen You   (Jim Morrison)

My eyes have seen you
My eyes have seen you
My eyes have seen you
Stand in your door
Meet inside
Show me some more
Show me some more
Show me some more

My eyes have seen you
My eyes have seen you
My eyes have seen you
Turn and stare
Fix your hair
Move upstairs
Move upstairs
Move upstairs

My eyes have seen you
My eyes have seen you
My eyes have seen you
Free from disguise
Gazing on a city under
Television skies
Television skies
Television skies

My eyes have seen you
My eyes have seen you
Eyes have seen you
Let them photograph your soul
Memorize your alleys on an
Endless roll
Endless roll
Endless roll
Endless roll
Endless roll
Endless roll
Endless roll
Endless roll
Endless roll
Endless roll

Endless roll
Endless roll
Endless roll
Endless roll
Endless roll
Endless roll
Endless roll

I Can't See Your Face In My Mind   (Jim Morrison)

I can't see your face in my mind
I can't see your face in my mind
Carnival dogs consume the lines
Can't see your face in my mind

Don't you cry
Baby, please don't cry
And don't look at me
with your eyes

I can't seem to find the right lie
I can't seem to find the right lie
Insanity's horse adorns the sky
Can't seem to find the right lie

Carnival dogs consume the lines
Can't see your face in my mind

Don't you cry
Baby, please don't cry
I won't need your picture
until we say goodbye

When The Music's Over   (Jim Morrison)

Yeah, come on

Yeah!!

When the music's over
When the music's over, *yeah…*
When the music's over
Turn out the lights
Turn out the lights
Turn out the light
Yeah, yeah...

When the music's over
When the music's over
When the music's over
Turn out the lights
Turn out the lights
Turn out the light

Well, the music is your special friend
Dance on fire as it intends
Music is your only friend
Until the end
Until the end
Until the end
Aahh, love – fuck you in the ass, baby, yeah…

Cancel my subscription to the
Resurrection,
Send my credentials to the
House of Detention
I got some friends inside.

The face in the mirror won't stop,
The girl in the window won't drop,
A feast of friends –
"Alive!" she cried,
Waiting for me
Outside!

Before I sink
into the big sleep,
I want to hear,
I want to hear
the scream
of the butterfly.

Come back, baby
Back into my arm

We're getting tired of hanging around,
Waiting around with our heads to the ground

I hear a very gentle sound

Very near, yet very far
Very soft, yeah, very clear
Come today,
Come today.

What have they done to the earth, *yeah*
What have they done to our fair sister
Ravaged and plundered
and ripped her and bit her
Stuck her with knives
in the side of the dawn
And tied her with fences
and dragged her down

I hear a very gentle sound,
With your ear down to the ground

We want the world
and we want it –
now

We want the world
and we want it –
now

Now?

Now!!

Persian night, babe!
See the light, babe!
Save us!
Jesus!
Save us!

So when the music's over
When the music's over, *yeah…*
When the music's over
Turn out the lights
Turn out the lights
Turn out the light

Well, the music is your special friend
Dance on fire as it intends
Music is your only friend
Until the end
Until the end
Until the end!

music's over   cont.

Come back, baby
Back into my arm

We're getting tired of waiting around,
Just hanging around w/ our heads
                              to the ground

I hear a very gentle sound

Very near, yet very far
Very soft, yet very clear
Come today,
Come today.

What have they done to the earth
What have they done to our fair sister
Ravaged & plundered &
& ripped her & bit her
Stuck her knives
in the side of the dawn
Tied her w/ fences
and
dragged her down

I hear a very gentle sound,
w/ your ear down to the ground

(over)

STRANGE DAYS

Strange days have found us
Strange days have tracked us down
They're going to destroy
Our casual joys.
We shall go on playing
Or find a new town.

Strange eyes fill strange rooms
Voices will signal their tired end
The hostess is grinning
Her guests sleep from sinning
Hear me talk of sin
And you know this is it.

Strange days have found us
And through their strange hours
We linger alone,
Bodies confused,
Memories misused,
As we run from the day
To a strange night of stone.

YOU'RE LOST LITTLE GIRL

You're lost little girl
You're lost little girl
You're lost
Tell me who
Are you?

I think that you know what to do,
Impossible? Yes, but it's true.
I think that you know what to do—
I'm sure that you know what to do.

LOVE ME TWO TIMES

Love me two times, baby
Love me twice today
Love me two times, girl
I'm goin' away.
One for tomorrow,
One just for today,
Love me two times—
I'm goin' away.

Love me one time—
I could not speak,
Love me one time
Yeah, my knees got weak,
But love me two times, girl
Last me all through the week.
Love me two times—
I'm goin' away.

Oh, yes

Love me two times, babe
Love me twice today
Love me two times, babe
'Cause I'm goin' away.
Love me two times, girl
One for tomorrow,
One just for today
Love me two times
I'm goin' away.

UNHAPPY GIRL

Unhappy girl,
Left all alone
Playing solitaire
Playing warden to your soul
You are locked in a prison
Of your own
devise.
And you can't believe
What it does to me,
To see you
Crying.

Unhappy girl,
Tear your web away
Saw thru all your bars
Melt your cell today
You are caught
in a prison
of your own
devise.

Unhappy girl,
Fly fast away
Don't miss your chance
To swim in mystery
You are dying
in a prison
Of your own
devise.

HORSE LATITUDES

When the still sea conspires an armor
And her sullen and aborted
Currents breed tiny monsters,
True sailing is dead.

Awkward instant
And the first animal is jettisoned,
Legs furiously pumping
Their stiff green gallop,
And heads bob up
Poise
Delicate
Pause
Consent
In mute nostril agony
Carefully refined
And sealed over.

MOONLIGHT DRIVE

Let's swim to the moon
Let's climb through the tide
Penetrate the evening
That the city sleeps to hide
Let's swim out tonight, love
It's our turn to try
Parked beside the ocean
On our moonlight drive.

Let's swim to the moon
Let's climb through the tide
Surrender to the waiting worlds
That lap against our side.
Nothing left open
And no time to decide.
We've stepped into a river
On our moonlight drive.

Let's swim to the moon
Let's climb through the tide
You reach a hand to hold me
But I can't be your guide.
It's easy to love you
As I watch you glide.
We're falling through wet forests
On our moonlight drive.

Come on, baby, gonna take a little ride
Goin' down by the ocean side
Gonna get real close
Get real tight
Baby gonna drown tonight.
Goin' down, down, down.

PEOPLE ARE STRANGE

People are strange when you're a stranger,
Faces look ugly when you're alone.
Women seem wicked when you're unwanted,
Streets are uneven when you're down.

When you're strange
Faces come out of the rain
When you're strange
No one remembers your name
When you're strange
When you're strange
When you're strange.

MY EYES HAVE SEEN YOU

My eyes have seen you
Stand in your door
When we meet inside
Show me some more.

My eyes have seen you
Turn and stare
Fix your hair
Move upstairs.

My eyes have seen you
Free from disguise
Gazing on a city under
Television skies.

PRINTED
IN
U.S.A.

My eyes have seen you
Let them photograph your soul
Memorize your alleys
On an endless roll.

I CAN'T SEE YOUR FACE IN MY MIND

I can't see your face in my mind
Carnival dogs
Consume the lines
Can't see your face in my mind.

Don't you cry.
Baby, please don't cry—
And don't look at me
With your eyes.

I can't seem to find the right lie
Insanity's horse
Adorns the sky
Can't seem to find the right lie.

Carnival dogs
Consume the lines
Can't see your face in my mind.

Don't you cry.
Baby, please don't cry.
I won't need your picture
Until we say goodbye.

WHEN THE MUSIC'S OVER

When the music's over
Turn out the lights.

The music is your special friend
Dance on fire as it intends
Music is your only friend
Until the end.

Cancel my subscription to the
Resurrection,
Send my credentials to the
House of Detention
I got some friends inside.

The face in the mirror won't stop,
The girl in the window won't drop,

A feast of friends—
"Alive!" she cried,
Waiting for me
Outside!

Before I sink
Into the big sleep,
I want to hear
the scream
of the butterfly.

Come back, baby
Back into my arm.
We're getting tired of waiting around,
Waiting around
with our heads
to the ground.

I hear a very gentle sound.

What have they done to the earth?
What have they done to our fair sister?
Ravaged and plundered
and ripped her and bit her
Stuck her with knives
in the side of the dawn
and tied her with fences
and dragged her down.

I hear a very gentle sound,
With your ear down to the ground—
We want the world and we want it
Now!

Persian night!
See the light!
Save us!
Jesus!
Save us!

So when the music's over,
Turn out the lights.

The music is your special friend
Dance on fire as it intends
Music is your only friend
Until the end
Until the end
Until
THE END!

elektra

EKS-74014

Hullabaloo, USA, 19 July 1968
Waiting For The Sun

It's a very interesting record, much happier and far less demonic. The parts that I like the best are the ones that contain the least Morrison. His mannerisms could so easily solidify into self-parody. Although he limits himself to two screams on WAITING FOR THE SUN, both of them sound a bit ridiculous. The strongest songs, with one exception, are the ones on which Manzarek, Krieger and Densmore come to the forefront. *Winter-time Love* and *Spanish Caravan* feature some beautiful instrumental work. My other favorite, *My Wild Love*, sounds like an English ballad chanted unaccompanied in a gospel style. All three sound almost nothing like The Doors of old. *Hello, I Love You* sounds like The Kinks.

There isn't any long song on WAITING FOR THE SUN. No sequel to *The End* and *When the Music's Over*. *Not To Touch The Earth* seems to be a kind of compressed version of them both at 3:54. The old snake crawls again and not too effectively. I think that they ought to retire him anyway. Or you could combine *Five to One* – which at first sounds like the theme song to a very bad movie called *Wild in the Streets* – with *Not To Touch The Earth* and come up with a sequel.

A lot of cynics thought that this album would be a disaster. That isn't my feeling at all. But I do think that Morrison's lyrics and stylization are wearing thin. I think that the other three Doors are much more solid, much more inventive. Manzarek is just brilliant on piano and organ. And Krieger finally gets to use his flamenco training on *Spanish Caravan*. The worst song on the whole LP is *The Unknown Soldier*. It manages to highlight everything bad about the group in the short space of 3:10. But I certainly don't think that WAITING FOR THE SUN is a disaster.

Los Angeles Times, USA, 4 August 1968
The Doors Find Love

The new album from The Doors, WAITING FOR THE SUN, is that difficult third LP which seems to thwart a number of contemporary pop groups.

The Doors have succeeded. Their first two LPs, THE DOORS and STRANGE DAYS, were quite similar both in structure and in mood. Each contained an eleven-minute fantasy number and some shorter songs whose fabric was trimmed from nightmarish visions and sexual images. Both were more grotesque than pretty. Both also were powerful enough to establish The Doors as the hottest group in the United States.

WAITING FOR THE SUN contains the fewest snakes, the least ugliness, the lowest number of freaks and monsters, and the smallest amount of self-indulgent mysticism of the trio of Doors' LPs. They have traded terror for beauty and the success of the swap is a tribute to their talent and originality.

Rolling Stone, USA, 28 September 1968
Waiting For The Sun

Listening to the new Doors' album reminded me of how good the first Doors album was; yet after a year and a half of Jim Morrison's posturing one might logically hope for some sort of musical growth, and if the new record isn't really terrible, it isn't particularly exciting either. The group, as always, is tight: Manzarek does some nice things on keyboards and Krieger acquits himself quite capably on guitar; the rhythm section (particularly Densmore) leaves something to be desired in the way of swing, but at least everybody is together.

The album's songs vacillate between the trivial and the neo-Freudian, reaching in some cases new depths as far as lyrics go: "Summer's almost gone / Summer's almost gone / We had some good times / But they're gone…" But the real problem is Morrison, for The Doors have come to be structured around him: there are no extended solos to speak of, which is a pity considering Manzarek's not inconsiderable skill. On this album Morrison doesn't seem to sing as well as on the first Doors' release, but more important is his lack of subtlety.

There are of course some good tracks: *Spanish Caravan* features some beautiful Krieger classical guitar work, and is well-arranged; *Not To Touch The Earth* (part of a longer 'theater piece', *The Celebration of the Lizard*) also has its moments, and in spite of its lyrics the music to *Summer's Almost Gone* is highly evocative, with Krieger's slippery bottleneck guitar effectively embellishing the song. *Hello, I Love You* and *We Could Be So Good Together* are pretty thin fare, while the marriage of Morrison with the work song *My Wild Love* is somewhat awkward. There is some nice Manzarek harpsichord on *Wintertime Love* (a waltz), but nothing of real substance, and Morrison shows on *Yes, The River Knows* that he is incapable of sustaining a ballad. Then there is the album's 'hard' rhythm and blues number, *Five To One*, where Morrison manages to sound like a combination of Barry Melton, Wolfman Jack and Conway Twitty while the rhythm section chugs through the changes.

WAITING FOR THE SUN is a respectable, if unimpressive, third album; it at least represents an advance over STRANGE DAYS (which had the knack of sounding like the first Doors album, only not as good). Nevertheless The Doors are not a particularly exciting hard rock band and Morrison is something like rock music's equivalent to Rod McKuen. Whether all this adds up to the praise that has been heaped on The Doors in some circles is open to question. As for the music, great rock it isn't – but then Morrison is supposedly our generation's sex symbol. Anyway the cover is pretty.

Crawdaddy!, USA, October 1968
Banging Away At The Doors Of Convention

WAITING FOR THE SUN, released one year after their initial arrival on the big scene, is the inheritor of so many heirlooms, bonds and old furniture rattling around the attic and closets of The Doors' house of success. *Hello, I Love You*, with its pale Kinks-imitation and its weird touches recalls the *Twentieth Century Fox* vein: lyrics denuded, sparse, unimaginably direct. *Love Street* and *Summer's Almost Gone* introduce novelty: The happy Doors, as Manzarek, ever the ascetic at the keyboard, lilts a melody not unlike a permanent wave.

On the third album there is ever-present the nostalgia factor. Nothing The Doors do can remain untainted by sex – they are far removed from the sand and the sun, and they are very much the captives of their audience. The Doors, more consciously than any other rock performers, deal in recollection, in *leitmotiv*, in echo. They are hung on the possibility of thematic integrity. They relate to themselves, their own on-going achievement. They accomplished, through one album, the reality of an instant recognition, and the third album is merely an extended revelation. *We Could Be So Good Together* rises out of the ashes of Morrison's vocal stance in *Take It As It Comes*. Where once they set about instigating an expectation, now they only fulfill it, as though they were the only ones to be awaited.

Disc and Music Echo, GB, 14 September 1968
Doors: hard as an uncut diamond

Of course The Doors are as worthy of serious attention as The Beatles, The Stones or anyone else you care to mention. Moreover they are the biggest group in the States as of three months ago, with a wealth of number ones, three gold albums and just about every other accolade a grateful nation can bestow on its favorite group.

Musically they have always been utterly superb, and on this, their third album, they've improved immeasurably. It's sheer driving music, as hard as an uncut diamond, with Morrison's hoarse, powerful vocal pounding out over quite alarming organ, sublime guitar and crashing drums. Jim Morrison's lyrics, always powerful, on this album prove him the near-equal of giants like Bob Dylan, John Lennon and Dr. John Creux. Just listen to *Five To One*, a call to arms for this generation: "They got the guns, but we got the numbers!"

The Doors will become as much a symbol of the next three years as The Stones or Beatles did in the last three or four – at the moment in the States only, but if anything can break them here, this album should be it.

Hello, I Love You   (Jim Morrison)

Hello, I love you
Won't you tell me your name?
Hello, I love you
Let me jump in your game
Hello, I love you
Won't you tell me your name?
Hello, I love you
Let me jump in your game

She's walking down the street
Blind to every eye she meets
Do you think you'll be the guy
To make the queen of the angels sigh?

Hello, I love you
Won't you tell me your name?
Hello, I love you
Let me jump in your game
Hello, I love you
Won't you tell me your name?
Hello, I love you
Let me jump in your game

She holds her head so high
Like a statue in the sky
Her arms are wicked and her legs are long
When she moves my brain screams out this song

Sidewalk crouches at her feet
Like a dog that begs for something sweet
Do you hope to make her see you fool?
Do you hope to pluck this dusky jewel?

Hello!   Hello!
Hello!   Hello!
Hello!   Hello!
Hello!   Hello!
Hello!   Hello!
Hello!   Hello!
Hello!   Hello!

I want you   *Yeah...*   Hello!
                              Hello!   Hello!
I need my baby   Hello!
                              I miss you   Hello!
Love   Hello!
my girl   I need you   Hello!
Yeah...   Hello!
                              Love my baby   Hello!
Ha!   *Uh-huh*   Hello!
Hello!   Hello!
Hello!   Hello!
Hello!   Hello!
Hello!   Hello!

Love Street   (Jim Morrison)

She lives on Love Street
Lingers long on Love Street
She has a house and garden
I would like to see what happens

She has robes and she has monkeys
Lazy diamond-studded flunkies
She has wisdom and knows what to do
She has me and she has you

She has wisdom and knows what to do
She has me and she has you

I see you live on Love Street
There's the store where the creatures meet
I wonder what they do in there
Summer Sunday and a year

I guess I like it fine
So far

She lives on Love Street
Lingers long on Love Street
She has a house and garden
I would like to see what happens

Not To Touch The Earth   (Jim Morrison)

Not to touch the earth
Not to see the sun
Nothing left to do, but
Run Run Run
Let's run
Let's run

House upon the hill
Moon is lying still
Shadows of the trees
Witnessing the wild breeze
Come on baby run with me
Let's run

Run with me
Run with me
Run with me
Let's run

The mansion is warm, at the top of the hill
Rich are the rooms and the comforts there
Red are the arms of luxuriant chairs
And you won't know a thing till you get inside

Dead president's corpse in the driver's car
The engine runs on glue and tar
Come on along, not going very far
To the East to meet the Czar

Run with me
Run with me
Run with me
Let's run
Wow!

Some outlaws lived by the side of a lake
The minister's daughter's in love with the snake
Who lives in a well by the side of the road
Wake up, girl, we're almost home
Yeah, come on!

We should see the gates by morning
We should be inside by evening

Not To Touch The Earth

Not to touch the earth
Not to see the sun
Nothing left to do, but
Run Run Run
Let's run
Let's run

House upon the hill / moon is lying still
Shadows of the trees / witnessing the wild breeze
C'mon baby run w/ me
Let's run
Let's run

Run w/ me (3)
Let's run

The mansion is warm, at the top of the hill
Rich are the rooms & the comforts there
Red are the arms of luxuriant chairs
And you won't know a thing til you get inside

Dead president's corpse in the driver's car
The engine runs on glue & tar
C'mon along, we're not going very far
To the East to meet the Czar

over

Sun Sun Sun
Burn Burn Burn
Soon Soon Soon
Moon – Moon – Moon
I will get you
Soon!
Soon!
Soon!

I am the Lizard King
I can do anything

Summer's Almost Gone   (Jim Morrison)

Summer's almost gone
Summer's almost gone
Almost gone
Yeah, it's almost gone
Where will we be
when the summer's gone?

Morning found us calmly unaware
Noon burned gold into our hair
At night we swam the laughing sea
When summer's gone
where will we be?

Where will we be?
Where will we be?

Morning found us calmly unaware
Noon burned gold into our hair
At night we swam the laughing sea
When summer's gone
where will we be?

Summer's almost gone
Summer's almost gone
We had some good times
But they're gone
The winter's coming on
Summer's almost gone

Wintertime Love   (Robby Krieger)

Wintertime winds blow cold this season
Falling in love I'm hoping to be
Wind is so cold, is that the reason
Keeping you warm, your hands touching me

Come with me, dance, my dear
Winter's so cold this year
You are so warm, my wintertime love to be

Wintertime winds, blue and freezing
Coming from northern storms in the sea
Love has been lost, is that the reason
Trying so desperately to be free

Ah, come with me, dance, my dear
Winter's so cold this year
You are so warm, my wintertime love to be

Come with me, dance, my dear
Winter's so cold this year
You are so warm, my wintertime love to be

The Unknown Soldier   (Jim Morrison)

Wait until the war is over
And we're both a little older
The Unknown Soldier

Breakfast where the news is read
Television, children fed
Unborn living, living dead
Bullet strikes the helmet's head

And it's all over
for the Unknown Soldier
It's all over
for the Unknown Soldier
Uh-huh...

Go! Go! Go to Viet Nam!
Go! Go! Go to Viet Nam!
Go! Go! Go to Viet Nam!

Company halt!
Present arms!

Make a grave for the Unknown Soldier
Nestled in your hollow shoulder
The Unknown Soldier

Breakfast where the news is read
Television, children fed
Bullet strikes the helmet's head

And it's all over
The war is over
It's all over
War is over

It's all over, babe!
All over, baby!
Oh!
Over, yeah!
All over, baby!
Aahh, haha!
All over!

All over, babe!
Oh!
Oh yeah!
All over!
All over

Yeah...
Yeah...

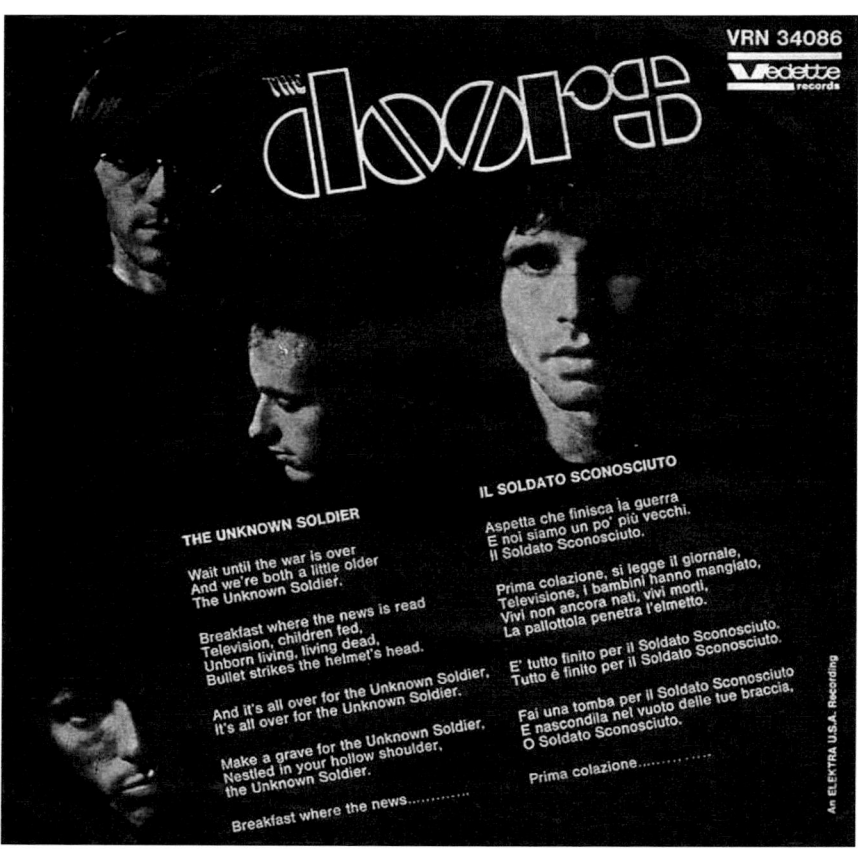

Spanish Caravan (Robby Krieger)

Carry me, caravan, take me away
Take me to Portugal, take me to Spain
Andalusia with fields full of grain
I have to see you again and again

Take me, Spanish caravan
Yes, I know you can

Trade winds find galleons lost in the sea
I know where treasure is waiting for me
Silver and gold in the mountains of Spain
I have to see you again and again

Take me, Spanish caravan
Yes, I know you can

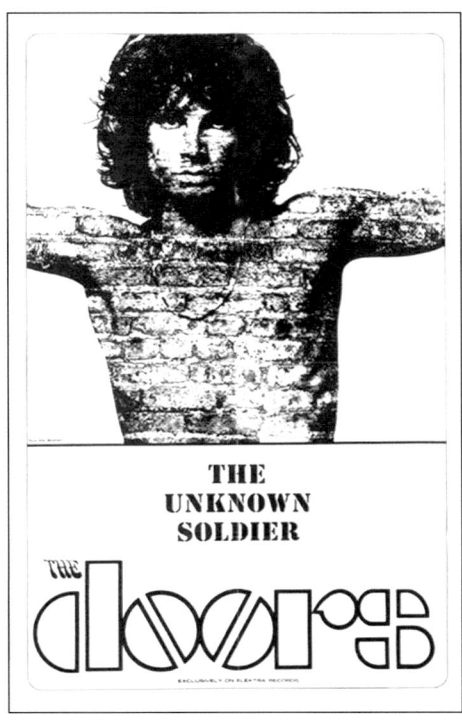

My Wild Love   (Jim Morrison)

My wild love went riding
She rode all the day
She rode to the devil
and asked him to pay

The devil was wiser
It's time to repent
He asked her to give back
the money she spent

My wild love went riding
She rode to the sea
She gathered together
some shells for her hair

She rode and she rode on
She rode for a while
Then stopped for an evening
and laid her head down

She rode on to Christmas
She rode to the farm
She rode to Japan
and re-entered a town

By this time the weather
had changed one degree
She asked for the people
to let her go free

My wild love is crazy
She screams like a bird
She moans like a cat
when she wants to be heard

My wild love went riding
She rode for an hour
She rode and she rested
And then she rode on
Right, come on!

We Could Be So Good Together   (Jim Morrison)

We could be so good together
Yeah, so good together
We could be so good together
Yeah, we could
I know we could

Tell you lies
I tell you wicked lies
Tell you lies
Tell you wicked lies

Tell you about the world that we'll invent
Wanton world without lament
Enterprise
Expedition
Invitation and invention

Yeah, so good together
Ah, so good together
We could be so good together
Yeah, we could
Know we could
Alright!

We could be so good together
Yeah, so good together
We could be so good together
Yeah, we could
Know we could

Tell you lies
Tell you wicked lies
Tell you lies
Tell you wicked lies

The time you wait subtracts from joy
Beheads the Angels you destroy
Angels fight
Angels cry
Angels dance and Angels die

Yeah, so good together
Ah, but so good together
We could be so good together
Yeah, we could
Know we could

Yes, The River Knows   (Robby Krieger)

Please believe me
The river told me
Very softly
Want you to hold me

Free fall flow river flow
On and on it goes
Breathe under water till the end
Free fall flow river flow
On and on it goes
Breathe under water till the end

Yes, the river knows

Please believe me
If you don't need me
I'm going but I need a little time
I promised I would drown myself
in mystic heated wine

Please believe me
The river told me
Very softly
Want you to hold me

I'm going but I need a little time
I promised I would drown myself
in mystic heated wine

Free fall flow river flow
On and on it goes
Breathe under water till the end
Free fall flow river flow
On and on it goes
Breathe under water till the end

Five To One   (Jim Morrison)

Yeah, come on
Love my girl
She's looking good
Feel
Come on
One more

Five to one, baby, one in five
No one here gets out alive
Now you get yours, baby, I'll get mine
Gonna make it, baby, if we try

The old get old and the young get stronger
May take a week and it may take longer
They got the guns but we got the numbers
Gonna win, yeah, we're taking over
Come on!

Right!

Your ballroom days are over, baby
Night is drawing near
Shadows of the evening
Crawl across the years

You walk across the floor with a flower in your hand
Trying to tell me no one understands
Trading your hours for a handful of dimes
Gonna make it, baby, in our prime

Get together one more time
Get together one more time   *Get together one more time*
Get together one more time   *Get together one more time*
Get together...   *Get together one more time*
Uh, haha

Get together one more time!   *Get together one more time*
Get together one more time!   *Get together one more time*
Get together one more time   *Get together one more time*
Get together one more time   *Get together one more time*

Get together
Gotta
Get together
Gotta
Get together
Gotta...
(...)
Aahh, whoah!

Hey, come on, honey, you
go along home and wait for
me, baby, I'll be there in just
a little while. You see, I got to
go out in this car with these
people and get... yeah...

Get together one more time!
Get together one more time!

Get together
Gotta
Get together
Gotta
Get together
Gotta...

Take me up into the mountains and...
Hahahahahahahahaha

Love my girl
She's looking good
Looking real good
Love you
Come on

Feel!
Yeah!
Come on!
Wow!

Get together one more time

Get together one more time

Get together one more time

Get together one more time

Get together one more time

Get together one more time

Get together one more time

Get together one more time
Get together one more time

Get together one more time

Get together one more time

Get together one more time

Get together one more time

Get together one more time

Get together one more time

THE DOORS/COMPLETE

A deluxe book of words, music, guitar chords, photographs, text and all their songs.

Jim Morrison/vocals
Ray Manzarek/keyboards
Robby Krieger/guitar
John Densmore/drums

Music Sales Corporation/$7.95

THE **P** PARADOX MUSIC GROUP
With DOORS MUSIC

Disc and Music Echo, GB, 1 February 1969
Doors Surprise With An Ordinary Love Song

Touch Me – I must say it's quite a thought to get together, of Jim Morrison singing touching little words about ordinary everyday things like falling in love over sweet strings – but there, odd things happen these days, and that's exactly what he does on this record. The combination of this and the typical Doors drum insistence and loosely-knit backing is unnerving to say the least. But it all works in an odd way, and having picked up ordinary pop fans with *Hello, I Love You* I should think they'd pick up a few more with this. Which confirms the feeling – on hearing it more than twice – that this will be a hit.

?, GB, May 1969
Sinful Jim

Doors: *Wishful Sinful*. Whispering Jim 'trousers down' Morrison doing his sexy sinful vocal on the group's current U.S. hit which is very much The Doors' sound as before but without the urgency or the excitement of their *Hello, I Love You* hit. Personally I find Morrison's attempts at being a male Marilyn Monroe rather amusing, but in danger of becoming boring. As *Touch Me* didn't happen, and this is in the same vein, I can't forecast a hit.

?, GB, May 1969
Wishful Sinful

The sound's getting bigger and bigger, I think the house will explode in a minute. (Laughs and shakes his head). It's one of the most uncommercial records I've ever heard in my life. Who is it? Oh! God, it's terrible. The sound is just dreadful. Are people really digging this in the States? The Doors... My God, that is a surprise. The orchestral arrangement sounds very clever and is very well done. It sounds like someone's singing very badly. I hope I never meet Jim Morrison.

?, GB, May 1969
Wishful Sinful

The Doors are doing some very weird things on record these days that completely throw me. Here's Jim Morrison's rather weird voice with some great sweeping strings – they're the only thing that give you a clue to the actual melody – and *Mr. Tambourine Man* guitar. An odd combination of a basically good song and all those odd notes that suddenly crop up on Doors songs and sound as though they have no right being there at all.

?, GB, May 1969
I'm worried about Jim, Morrison that is

Doors: *Wishful Sinful*. There is a strange desperation in Jim Morrison's voice, and a certain strength, whatever one may think of his stage image. This is a fine production, making intelligent use of strings, and an attractive tune. Morrison emotes with sincerity, which makes his heavily publicized bouts of exposure all the more tragic. Surely Doors don't need all that?

?, GB, 2 August 1969
So what's so great about these Doors?

Doors: *Tell All The People*. Don't know why it is, but thousands of people absolutely rave about The Doors, but – try as I may – I remain more or less indifferent. This latest disc is fairly pleasant, but not outstanding, though I'm obliged to rate it as a possible for the Chart because of the group's widespread popularity. It's a punchy rhythmic ballad, in which the lead singer displays a powerful resonance and shocking diction, while the other boys chip in with colorful harmonies. The tune is simple and repetitive, which means it registers quickly, but also runs the risk of becoming monotonous. Top marks to Paul Harris' orchestral arrangement, with fanfare brass prominent – it's a really magnificent backing and, for me, this alone is worth the price of the disc.

Melody Maker, GB, 4 October 1969
The Soft Parade

The album is padded with single tracks and runs a little short on time. Morrison sings in pleasant style and the group play reasonably well.

Rolling Stone, USA, 23 August 1969
The Soft Parade

A front page ad in *Billboard* says it: "Initial orders promise it will attain the instant solid gold status of their first three albums." It looks like it will, but not because anyone listened to the record.

Alternate suggested titles for THE SOFT PARADE would be *The Worst of the Doors*, *Kick Out the Doors*, or best, *The Soft Touch*.

THE SOFT PARADE is worse than infuriating, it's sad. It's sad because one of the most potentially moving forces in rock has allowed itself to degenerate. A trite word, but true.

THE SOFT PARADE represents a clear and present decline in musicianship. This is quite apart from stage showmanship, or even 'drama'. The Doors are obviously more potent than ever. But The Doors are a rock group, and at heart a rock group must produce vital, listenable, interesting music, or the rest is just so many limp wicks waving in the Miami breeze.

And this gorgeous-looking album is not vital, not very listenable and is certainly not interesting. It sounds for all the world like the stuff they had the good sense to leave off their first albums. The weaknesses cannot be palmed off as experimentation, because, despite the addition of strings and horns, it's just the same. The same but worse.

Ok, there are two un-Doors-like songs, both written by Robby Krieger. *Touch Me* and *Tell All The People* are horn string showpieces for the resonant baritone of Jim Morrison that *aren't* the worst of The Doors. They're the worst of Jerry Vale or the worst of Andy Williams. While The Doors' *reductio-ad-absurdum* poetry could usually be disguised by invigorating (if not very convincing) emotion, these damn songs stick that idiocy right up front and surround it with the most cliché-ridden sounds this side of the 101 Strings.

The remainder of the songs sound like The Doors alright, but they're pale shadows of their earlier works. The Doors' power is also their weakness. They have had from the beginning, and still have, one of the cleanest, most solid and, above all, most recognizable sounds in rock. Part of this is the Morrison power, but the other Doors are equally responsible. There is rarely any doubt that you're listening to The Doors. It's a great sound, a successful sound, but it forces a highly directional form of musical invention on The Doors and it is this that they have not been able to maintain. Instead they've just gone from excess to excess.

Runnin' Blue is a superb example. It's hard to imagine Doors' poetry getting more excessive than it's been, but listen to this: "Poor Otis dead and gone / Left me here to sing his song / Pretty little girl with the red dress on / Poor Otis dead and gone". Can you dig it? Or, better yet, *Do It*: "Please please listen to me children / Please please listen to me children / Please please listen to me children / Please please listen to me children / You are the ones who will rule the world".

And if, as Morrison himself says, the words don't count and the mood created is the important facet of The Doors' rock, then they've really bummed out on this one. The mood they've created is loud, dull boredom. There are some good images, some good musical licks, but it just isn't worth shuffling through the rest of this scree to find the few semi-precious stones.

What little good there is on the album is mostly in the title cut, *The Soft Parade*. But the thing is so mangled, so jammed together and frequently so silly that it's kind of hard to listen all through its 8:40 for the good.

With individual credit now being given for the songs, it's plain that Morrison's songs are better than Krieger's. But it's just the lesser of two evils.

In any case, with this album, The Doors appear to be in the final stages of musical constipation. Morrison admits that they haven't done any new material in three years, and unless something drastic happens, the next album ought to be an epitaph.

I highly recommend THE SOFT PARADE for those people who like to be bored to tears in order to make the time pass more slowly. Otherwise, don't bother.

New Musical Express, GB, 13 September 1969

Doors' music powerful

THE SOFT PARADE. The Doors are joined on some tracks by other musicians, but mainly it is the mystic merging of organ and guitar within the group that is the fascination of this intriguing set. The mood varies, too, from the heavy morbidity of *Shaman's Blues* to the fast trotting of *Easy Ride*, or the tuneful folksy inspirational *Tell All The People*. The background music is most effective on *Wild Child*, when Morrison sings in almost a monotone to lend more accent to the instrumental.

The title number, *The Soft Parade*, is written by Jim Morrison, almost 9 minutes of dramatics, starting out with him yelling: "You cannot petition the Lord with prayer". Then comes a quiet song with someone asking for soft asylum 'cause he can't make it any more. The music brightens and then goes weirder as Morrison tells us: "This is the best part of the trip". The main part is now sung and this builds up to a vocal battle and a strong voice finally declaring: "When all else fails we can whip the horses' eyes and make them sleep and cry". The lyric doesn't make much sense but it matches into the ever-increasing rhythm of the music. Powerful stuff. Morrison and Krieger have all composing credits between them.

Disc, USA, August 1969

Disc Albums Of The Week

THE SOFT PARADE. At last, the tightest record The Doors have produced: it's full of excitement and spontaneity, but with the sort of planning and precision that's been missing from so much of their work before now. *Runnin' Blue*, written by guitarist Robby Krieger, is only just over two minutes long, but it's a good little song, with sax solo and fiddle. *Wishful Sinful* confirms Krieger as a constructive songwriter. Throughout, Jim Morrison's vocals are sympathetic and driving. And it's as inventive an album as you'll find from the West Coast.

Tell All The People   (Robby Krieger)

Tell all the people that you see
Follow me
Follow me down

Tell all the people that you see
Set them free
Follow me down

You tell them they don't have to run
We're gonna pick up everyone
Come on, take me by my hand
Gonna bury all our troubles in the sand
Oh yeah

Can't you see the wonder at your feet
Your life's complete
Follow me down

Can't you see me growing, get your guns
The time has come
To follow me down

Follow me across the sea
Where milky babies seem to be
Molded flowing revelry
With the one that set them free

Tell all the people that you see
It's just me
Follow me down

Tell all the people that you see
Follow me
Follow me down

Tell all the people that you see
We'll be free
Follow me down

Tell all the people that you see
It's just me
Follow me down

Tell all the people that you see
Follow me
Follow me down

Follow me down
You got to follow me down
Follow me down

Tell all the people that you see
We'll be free
Follow me down

Tell all the people you see
Follow me
Got to follow me down

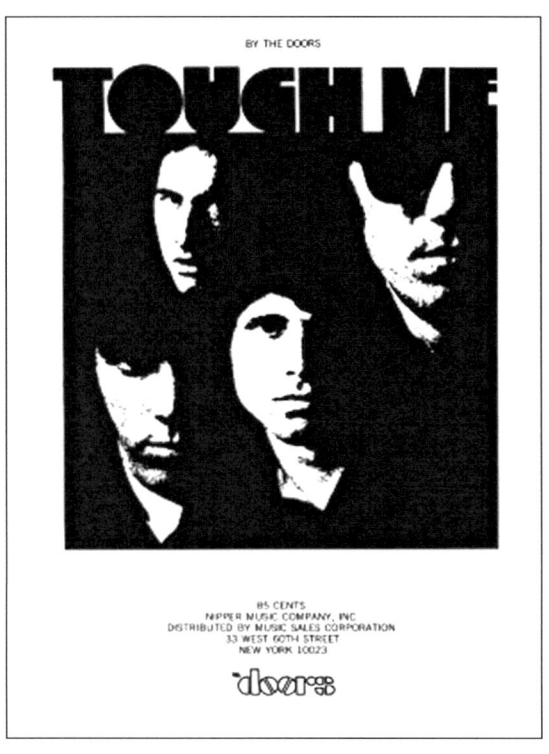

Touch Me   (Robby Krieger)

Yeah!

Come on, come on, come on, come on now
Touch me, babe
Can't you see that I am not afraid
What was that promise that you made
Why won't you tell me what she said
What was that promise that you made

Now, I'm gonna love you
Till the heavens stop the rain
I'm gonna love you
Till the stars fall from the sky
For you and I

Come on, come on, come on, come on now
Touch me, babe
Can't you see that I am not afraid
What was that promise that you made
Why won't you tell me what she said
What was that promise that you made

I'm gonna love you
Till the heavens stop the rain
I'm gonna love you
Till the stars fall from the sky
For you and I

I'm gonna love you
Till the heavens stop the rain
I'm gonna love you
Till the stars fall from the sky
For you and I

Stronger than dirt!

Shaman's Blues (Jim Morrison)

There will never be another one like you
There will never be another one
Who can do the things you do
Oh, will you give another chance
Will you try a little try
Please stop and you'll remember
We were together
Anyway...
All right

And if you have a certain evening
You could lend to me
I'd give it all right back to you
Know how it has to be
With you
I know your moods
And your mind
And your mind
And your mind
And your mind
And you're mine

Ah, will you stop to think and wonder
Just what you'll see
Out on the train-yard
Nursing penitentiary
It's gone
I cry
Out long

Go ahead, brother!

Did you stop to consider
How it will feel
Cold grinding grizzly-bear jaws
Hot on your heels
Do you often stop and whisper
In Saturday's shore:
"The whole world's a savior"
Who could ever, ever, ever, ever, ever, ever
Ask for more

Do you remember
Will you stop
Will you stop
The pain

And there will never be another one like you
There will never be another one
Who can do the things you do
Oh, will you give another chance
Will you try a little try
Please stop and you'll remember
We were together
Anyway...
All right

How you must *a*-think and wonder
How I must feel
Out on the meadows
While you're on the field
I'm alone
For you
And I cry

He's sweating, look at him
Optical promise, hahahaha
You'll be dead and in hell
before I'm born
Sure thing
Bride's maid
The only solution –
Isn't it amazing!

Do It   (Jim Morrison)

Hahahahahahaha
Yeah

Yeah, please me, yeah
Easy babe
Please, please

Please, please, listen to me, children
Please, please, listen to me, children
Please, please, listen to me, children
Said, please, please, listen to me, children
You are the ones who will rule the world

Listen to me, children
Listen to me, children
Please, please, listen to me, children
Please, please, listen to me, children
You are the ones who will rule the world
Ha!

You gotta please me
All night

Please, please, listen to me, children
Said, please, please, listen to me, children

Please!
Yeah, please me!
I'm asking you

Please, please, listen to me, children
Please, please, listen to me, children
Please, please, listen to me, children
Please, my children
Please, children
Please, children

Easy Ride   (Jim Morrison)

And I know
it will be
an easy ride
All right
And I know
it will be
an easy ride
Okay

The mask that you wore
My fingers would explore
Costume of control
Excitement soon unfolds

And I know
it will be
easy ride
Yeah...
Joy fought vaguely
with your pride
with your pride
Yeah...

Like polished stone
Like polished stone
I see your eyes
Like burning glass
Like burning glass
Hear you smile
Smile babe

The mask that you wore
My fingers would explore
Costume of control
Excitement soon unfolds

Hey!
Easy baby

Coda queen now be my bride
Rage in darkness by my side
Seize the summer in your pride
Take the winter in your stride
Let's ride – *yeah*

Easy
Easy
Easy
Easy
Easy
Easy
Easy
Yeah
Yeah
Ride

All right
(Come on!)

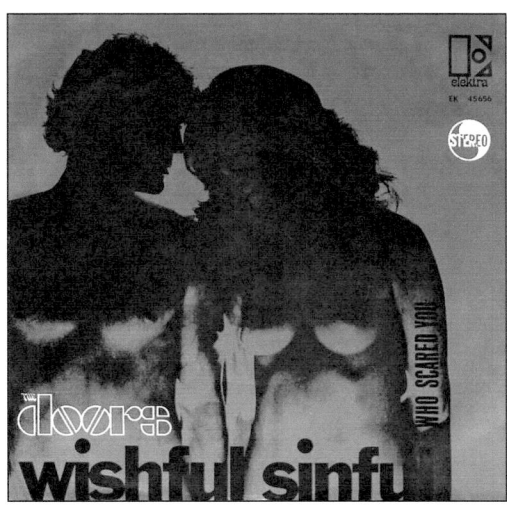

Wild Child   (Jim Morrison)

Alright!

Wild child
Full of grace
Savior of the human race
Your cool face

Natural child
Terrible child
Not your mother's or your
Father's child
You're our child
Screaming wild

An ancient lunatic reigns in the trees of the night
Hahahaha

With hunger at her heels
Freedom in her eyes
She dances on her knees
Pirate Prince at her side
Staring
Into
The hollow idol's eye

Wild child
Full of grace
Savior of the human race
Your cool face
Your cool face
Your cool face

Do you remember when we were in Africa?

Runnin' Blue   (Robby Krieger)

Poor Otis dead and gone
Left me here to sing his song
Pretty little girl with the red dress on
Poor Otis dead and gone

Yeah, back down, turn around slowly
Try it again
Remembering when
It was easy, try it again
Much too easy – remembering when

All right, look at my shoes
Not quite the walking blues
Don't fight, too much to lose
Can't fight the running blue

Well, I've got the running blues
Running away
Back to L.A.
Got to find the dock in the bay
Maybe find it back in L.A.

Running scared, running blue
Going so fast, what'll I do

Well, I've got the running blues
Running away
Back to L.A.
Got to find the dock in the bay
Maybe find it back in L.A.

All right, look at my shoes
Not quite the walking blues
Don't fight, too much to lose
Can't fight the running blue

All right, look at my shoes
Not quite the walking blues
Don't fight, too much to lose
Can't fight the running blue

Wishful Sinful   (Robby Krieger)

Wishful crystal
water covers
everything in blue
Cooling water

Wishful, sinful
Our love is beautiful to see
I know where I would like to be
Right back where I came

Wishful sinful wicked blue
Water covers you
Wishful sinful wicked you
Can't escape the blue

Magic rising
sun is shining
deep beneath the sea
But not enough for
you and me and sunshine
Love to hear the wind cry

Wishful, sinful
Our love is beautiful to see
I know where I would like to be
Right back where I came

Wishful sinful wicked blue
Water covers you
Wishful sinful wicked you
Can't escape the blue

Love to hear the wind cry
Love to hear you crying, *yeah*

The Soft Parade   (Jim Morrison)

When I was back there in seminary school
There was a person there
Who put forth the proposition
That you can petition the Lord with prayer
Petition the Lord with prayer
Petition the Lord with prayer

You cannot petition the Lord with prayer!

Can you give me sanctuary
I must find a place to hide
A place for me to hide

Can you find me soft asylum
I can't make it any more
The Man is at the door

Peppermint miniskirts, chocolate candy
Champion sax and a girl named Sandy

There's only four ways to get unraveled
One is to sleep and the other is travel

One is a bandit up in the hills
One is to love your neighbor till
his wife gets home

Catacombs
Nursery bones
Winter women growing stones
Carrying babies to the river

Streets and shoes
Avenues
Leather riders selling news

The Monk Bought Lunch

Hahaha,
he bought a little!

Yes, he did!

Wow!

This is the best
part of the trip
This is the trip
The best part
I really like

What did he say?

Yeah!

Yeah – right!

Pretty good, huh?

Ha!

Yeah, I'm proud
to be a part of
this number!

Successful hills are here to stay
Everything must be this way
Gentle street where people play
Welcome to the soft parade

All our lives we sweat and save
Building for a shallow grave
Must be something else, we say
Somehow to defend this place

Everything must be this way
Everything must be this way
Yeah

Aah – yeah!

The soft parade has now begun
Listen to the engines hum
People out to have some fun
Cobra on my left
Leopard on my right – *hey!*

Deer woman in a silk dress
Girls with beads around their necks
Kiss the hunter of the green vest
Who has wrestled before
with lions in the night

Out of sight!

The lights are getting brighter
The radio is moaning
Calling to the dogs
There are
still a few
animals
left out in the yard
But it's getting harder
to describe
sailors
to the underfed

Tropic corridor
Tropic treasure
What got us this far
to this mild equator?

We need someone or something new
Something else to get us through, *yeah*
Come on!

                                           Calling on
                                            the dogs
                                                        Calling on
                                                          the dogs

        But it's
        getting
        harder!   Calling on
                            Calling in   the dogs
                              the dogs

                                                Calling all
                                              the dogs

                            Calling on
                                the gods

You gotta
meet
me

Too late, baby!　　Still a few
　　　　　　　　animals

at the
crossroads

Too late!　　left out
in the yard
But it's
getting

Well, we're doing...　harder　　Gotta meet me　　*Whoah!*
we're doing great,
yeah!

at the edge
of town　　Tropic corridor
　　　　　Tropic treasure

Having a　　You'd better
good time!　　come
alone　　Outskirts of　　What got us this
A lot of fun!　　the city　　far to this mild
You and I　　　　　　equator?
Better　　We need
come alone　　someone or
something new

Better bring
your gun

Tropic　　Just you　　Something else
corridor　　and I　　to get
Tropic　　We're gonna　　us through,
treasure　　have some fun!　　*yeah*
What
got us this far

When all else fails　　And the
we can whip the horse's eyes　evening sky
and make them sleep
and cry

Who Scared You   (Jim Morrison)

Who scared you
Why were you born, my babe
Into time's arms
With all of your charms, my love
Why were you born
Just to play with me
To freak out or to be
beautiful, my dear

Load your head
Blow it up
Feel good, baby
Load your head
Blow it up
Feel good, baby
Ah!

Well, my room is so cold
You know you don't have to go, my babe
And if you warm it up right
I'm gonna love you tonight, my love
Well, I'm glad that we came
I hope you're feeling the same
Who scared you and why
were you born, please stay

I see a rider coming down the road
Got a burden, carrying a heavy load
One sack of silver and one bag of gold

This song was not included on the original LP THE SOFT PARADE. It was released on the B-side of the single *Wishful Sinful.*

TELL ALL THE PEOPLE †

Words & Music by Robbie Krieger

Tell all the people that you see
Follow me
Follow me down

Tell all the people that you see
Set them free
Follow me down

You tell them they don't have to run
We're gonna pick up every one
Come on, take me by my hand
Gonna bury all our troubles in the sand

Can't you see the wonder at your feet
Your life's complete
Follow me down

Can't you see me growing, get your guns
The time has come
To follow me down

Follow me across the sea
Where milky babies seem to be
Molded flowing revelry
With the one that set them free

Tell all the people that you see
It's just me
Follow me down

TOUCH ME*

Words & Music by Robbie Krieger

C'mon, c'mon, c'mon, c'mon now
Touch me babe
Can't you see that I am not afraid
What was that promise that you made
Why won't you tell me what she said
What was that promise that she made

I'm gonna love you
Till the heaven stops the rain
I'm gonna love you
Till the stars fall from the sky
For you and I

SHAMAN'S BLUES †

Words & Music by Jim Morrison

There will never be another one like you
There will never be another one
Who can do the things you do
Oh, will you give another chance
Will you try a little try
Please stop and you'll remember
We were together
Anyway . . . . . .

Now, if you have a certain evening
You could lend to me
I'd give it all right back to you
Know how it has to be
With you
I know your moods
and your mind

And your mind
And your mind
And your mind
And you're mine

Will you stop to think and wonder
Just what you'll see
Out on the train-yard
Nursing penitentiary
It's gone
I cry
Out long

Did you stop to consider
How it will feel
Cold grinding grizzly-bear jaws
Hot on your heels
Do you often stop and whisper
In Saturday's shore
That the whole world's a savior
Who could ever, ever, ever, ever
Ask for more

Do you remember
Will you stop
Will you stop
The pain . . . . .

There will never be another one like you
There will never be another one
Who can do the things you do
Oh, will you give another chance
Will you try a little try
Please stop and you'll remember
We were together
Anyway . . . . .

How you must to think and wonder
How I must feel
Out on the meadows
While you're on the field
I'm alone
For you
And I cry

(spoken)
He's sweatin'
Look at him
Optical promise
(You'll be dead and in hell
before I'm born.)
Sure thing
Bride's maid
The only solution—
Isn't it amazing!

DO IT †

Words & Music by Robbie Krieger-Jim Morrison

Please please listen to me children
Please please listen to me children
Please please listen to me children
Please please listen to me children
You are the ones who will rule the world

Please please listen to me children
Please please listen to me children
Please please listen to me children
Please my children
Please children

EASY RIDE †

Words & Music by Jim Morrison

And I know
It will be
An easy ride
And I know
It will be
an easy ride

The mask that you wore
My fingers would explore
The costume of control
Excitement soon unfolds

And I know
It will be
An easy ride
Joy fought vaguely
With your pride
With your pride

Like polished stone
Like polished stone
I see your eyes
Like burning glass
Like burning glass
I hear you smile
Smile babe

The mask that you wore
My fingers would explore
The costume of control
Excitement soon unfolds

And I know it will be
An easy ride

Coda queen—be my bride
Rage in darkness by my side
Seize the summer in your pride
Take the winter in your stride
Let's ride

WILD CHILD*

Words & Music by Jim Morrison

Wild child
Full of grace
Savior of the human race
Your cool face

Natural child
Terrible child
Not your mother or your
Father's child
You're our child
Screamin' wild

(An ancient lunatic reigns in the
                    trees of the night)

With hunger at her heels
And freedom in her eyes
She dances on her knees
Pirate Prince at her side
Staring
Into
The hollow idol's eyes

Wild child
Full of grace
Savior of the human race
Your cool face
Your cool face
Your cool face

(Do you remember when we were in Africa?)

RUNNIN' BLUE †

Words & Music by Robbie Krieger

Poor Otis dead and gone
Left me here to sing his song
Pretty little girl with the red dress on
Poor Otis dead and gone

Back down turn around slowly
Try it again—remembering when
It was easy, try it again
Much too easy—remembering when

All right, look at my shoes
Not quite the walkin' blues
Don't fight, too much to lose
Can't fight the runnin' blues

Well I've got the runnin' blues
Runnin' away, back to L.A.
Got to find the dock on the bay
Maybe find it back in L.A.

Runnin' scared, runnin' blue
Goin' so fast, what'll I do

Well I've got the runnin' blues
Runnin' away, back to L.A.
Got to find the dock on the bay
Maybe find it back in L.A.

All right, look at my shoes
Not quite the walkin' blues
Don't fight, too much to lose
Can't fight the runnin' blues

CHORUS (Repeat)

WISHFUL SINFUL*

Words & Music by Robbie Krieger

Wishful, crystal
Water covers everything in blue
Cooling water

Wishful, sinful
Our love is beautiful to see
I know where I would like to be
Right back where I came

Wishful, sinful wicked blue
Water covers you
Wishful sinful wicked you
Can't escape the blue

Magic, rising
Sun is shining deep beneath the sea
But not enough for you and me and sunshine
Love to hear the wind cry

Wishful, sinful wicked blue
Water covers you
Wishful sinful wicked you
Can't escape the blue

(Chorus—Repeat)

Love to hear the wind cry
Love to hear you cryin'

THE SOFT PARADE†

Words & Music by Jim Morrison

When I was back there in seminary school
There was a person there
Who put forth the proposition
That you can petition the Lord with prayer
Petition the Lord with prayer
Petition the Lord with prayer
You cannot petition the Lord with prayer!
•

Can you give me sanctuary
I must find a place to hide
A place for me to hide

Can you find me soft asylum
I can't make it any more
The man is at the door
•

Peppermint miniskirts, chocolate candy
Champion sax and a girl named Sandy

There's only four ways to get unraveled
One is to sleep and the other is travel

One is a bandit up in the hills
One is to love your neighbor till
His wife gets home
•

Catacombs, nursery bones
Winter women growing stones
(Carrying babies to the river)

Streets and shoes, avenues
Leather riders selling news

(The monk bought lunch)
•

Successful hills are here to stay
Everything must be this way
Gentle street where people play
Welcome to the soft parade

All our lives we sweat and save
Building for a shallow grave
Must be something else we say
Somehow to defend this place
(Everything must be this way
Everything must be this way)

The soft parade has now begun
Listen to the engines hum
People out to have some fun
A cobra on my left
Leopard on my right

Deer woman in a silk dress
Girls with beads around their necks
Kiss the hunter of the green vest
Who has wrestled before
With lions in the night

Out of sight!

The lights are getting brighter
The radio is moaning
Calling to the dogs
There are still a few animals
Left out in the yard
But it's getting harder
To describe
Sailors
To the underfed
•

Tropic corridor
Tropic treasure
What got us this far
To this mild Equator
We need someone or something new
Something else to get us through
•

Calling on the dogs
Calling on the dogs
Calling on the dogs
Calling in the dogs
Calling all the dogs
Calling on the gods

Meet me at the crossroads
Meet me at the edge of town
Outskirts of the city
Just you and I
And the evening sky
You'd better come alone
You'd better bring your gun
We're gonna have some fun!
•

When all else fails
We can whip the horses' eyes
And make them sleep
And cry . . . . .

ELEKTRA RECORDS
1855 Broadway
New York City 10023

PRINTED
IN
U. S. A.

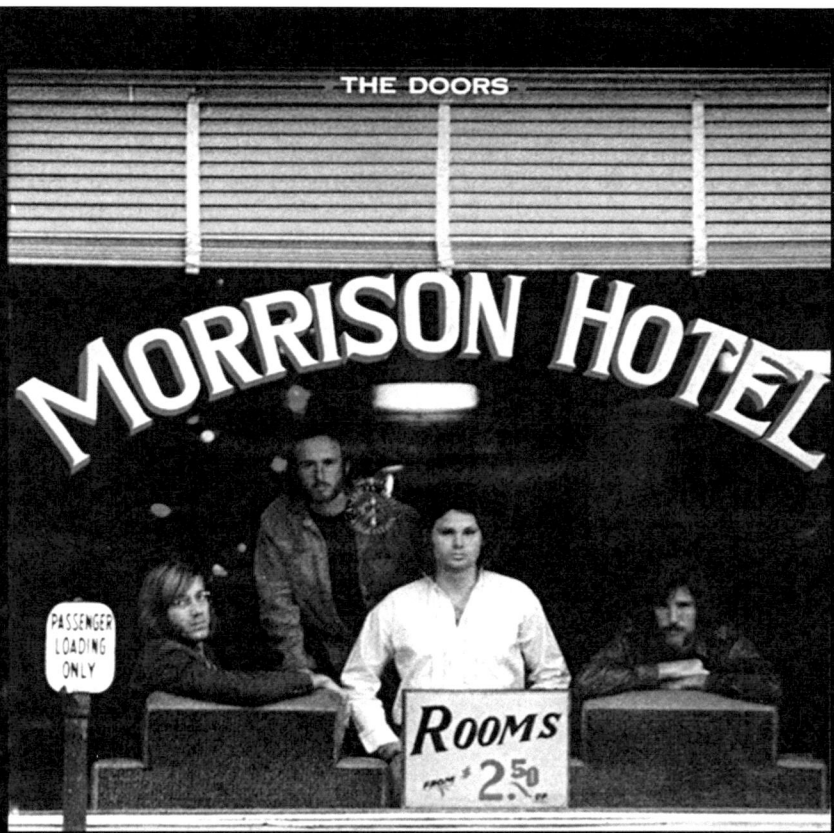

Rolling Stone, USA, 30 April 1970
Morrison Hotel

MORRISON HOTEL opens with a powerful blast of raw funk called *Road-house Blues*. It features jagged barrelhouse piano, fierce guitar, and one of the most convincing raunchy vocals Jim Morrison has ever recorded. This angry hard rock is that at which The Doors have always excelled, and given us so seldom, and this track is one of their very best ever, with brooding lyrics that ring chillingly, true.

From there on out, though, the road runs mainly downhill. It's really a shame, too, because somehow one held high expectations for this album and wanted so badly to believe it would be good that one was afraid to listen to it when it was finally released. The music bogs down in the kind of love mush and mechanical, stereotyped rock arrangements that have marred so much of The Doors' past music. *Blue Sunday* and *Indian Summer* are two more insipidly 'lyrical' pieces crooned in Morrison's most saccharine style. *Maggie M'Gill* is a monotonous progression in the vein of (but not nearly as interesting as) *Not To Touch The Earth*, and *You Make Me Real* is a thyroid burst of manufactured energy worthy of a thousand mediocre groups.

Admittedly, these are the worst tracks, and the rest ranges from the merely listenable to the harsh brilliance of *Roadhouse Blues* or the buoyant catchiness of *Land Ho!*, a chanty that sets you rocking and swaying on first listen and never fails to bring a smile every time it's repeated.

This could have been a fine album. But the unavoidable truth – and this seems to be an insurmountable problem for The Doors – is that so much of it is out of the same extremely worn cloth as the songs on all their other albums. It's impossible to judge it outside the context of the rest of their work. Robby Krieger's slithery guitar, and Manzarek's carnival-calliope organ work and whorehouse piano are the perfect complement to Morrison's rococo visions. But we've all been there before, not a few times, and their well of resources has proven a standing lake which is slowly drying up. Perhaps if they recombined into a different group, the brilliant promise of The Doors' first album and sporadic songs since might begin to be fulfilled, but for now they can only be truly recommended to those with a personal interest.

Jazz & Pop, USA, December 1970
Morrison Hotel

MORRISON HOTEL, The Doors' fifth album, is not what it seems. And anyone who tells you it's The Doors' return to that "good old rock 'n' roll" has either confused Fabian with Walt Whitman or has just been listening to The Moody Blues for too long.

The Doors have revived, even resurrected, a lot of lost arts in MORRISON HOTEL, which lyrically encompasses everything from poetry to parable, but in their hands, rock 'n' roll and all its magic have always been full of life and have never needed any special care.

Jim Morrison is a masterful songwriter, a provocative and inventive lyricist, a worthy composer, and a motherfucker of a singer. The best way to discover The Doors is to investigate the critical reaction against them. The people who dislike The Doors the most, in their attempts to demonstrate what's wrong with The Doors, never fail to point out just what it is that makes The Doors so great. The best picture of The Doors' brand of insanity is best drawn by the sane man who hates them. Only he can truly do justice to the group.

Morrison's performance, for instance, tends to be far more religious than it is political: Morrison has always been more a prophet than a pied piper, and if he cannot teach us how to live, he can at least teach us how not to live. Morrison has not so much attempted to destroy religion as he has attempted to replace it.

All Doors albums have been deeply autobiographical, especially the unjustly criticized THE SOFT PARADE LP, which was really on the whole an awful lot better than an awful lot of awful people wanted to have to admit. More than any other of the group's albums, THE SOFT PARADE is most specifically an album about The Doors and their meanings in our society.

MORRISON HOTEL, for all its flurries of autobiography, is really more directly an album about America. But like THE SOFT PARADE it is about you and me only by inference. Most of what has already been written about the album has been about the music, about how it is a return to the tight fury of early Doors music, of how it abounds with funk and guts and earth-energy. All this is true, and there can be little doubt that MORRISON HOTEL is one of the major musical events of Rock '70.

Los Angeles Free Press, USA, February 1970
The Doors

Achieving what no American rock group has yet to do, The Doors have copped their fifth straight gold record. The Elektra quartet's MORRISON HOTEL LP was certified as a $1,000,000-seller by the R.I.A.A. three days after its release. Other American groups, such as The Rascals and The Beach Boys have earned five gold disks. But The Doors are the first to chalk up five in a row.

Roadhouse Blues   (Jim Morrison)

(Yeah!)

A-keep your eyes on the road, your hand upon the wheel
Yeah, keep your eyes on the road, your hand upon the wheel
Yeah, we're going to the roadhouse, gonna have a real – a good time

Yeah, at the back of the roadhouse they got some bungalows
Yeah, at the back of the roadhouse they got some bungalows
And that's for the people who like to go down slow

Let it roll, baby, roll
Let it roll, baby, roll
Let it roll, baby, roll
Let it roll –
All night long, *yeah*

Do it, Robby, do it!

All right!

You gotta roll, roll, roll
You gotta thrill my soul
All right

Roll, roll, roll, roll
A-thrill my soul
(...)
Yeah, right!

Ashen Lady
Ashen Lady
Give up your vows
Give up your vows
Save our city!
Save our city!
Right now!

And I woke up this morning, I got myself a beer
Well, I woke up this morning and I got myself a beer
The future's uncertain and the end is always near

Let it roll, baby, roll
Let it roll, baby, roll
Let it roll, baby, roll
Let it roll – *yeah!*
All night long

There's blood in the streets
& its up to my ankles
Blood in the streets
& its up to my knee
Blood in the streets
of the town of chicago
Blood on the rise
& its following me –
Blood in the streets
runs a river of sadness
Blood in the streets
& its up to my thigh
The river runs red
down the legs of the city
The women are crying
red rivers of weeping

Waiting For The Sun   (Jim Morrison)

At first flash of Eden we race down to the sea
Standing there on freedom's shore

Waiting for the sun
Waiting for the sun
Waiting for the sun

Can't you feel it, now that spring has come
That it's time to live in the scattered sun

Waiting for the sun
Waiting for the sun
Waiting for the sun
Waiting for the sun

Waiting, waiting, waiting, waiting
Waiting, waiting, waiting, waiting

Waiting for you to come along
Waiting for you to hear my song
Waiting for you to come along, *yeah*
Waiting for you to tell me what went wrong

This is the strangest life I've ever known
Go-ahead!! What's the matter?!
Whoah...

Can't you feel it, now that spring has come
That it's time to live in the scattered sun

Waiting for the sun
Waiting for the sun
Waiting for the sun
Waiting for the sun

You Make Me Real   (Jim Morrison)

I really want you
Really do
Really need you, baby
God knows I do
'Cause I'm not real enough without you
Oh, what can I do?

You make me real
You make me feel like lovers feel
You make me throw away mistake and misery
Make me free, love, make me free
Aaah – come on!
Aaah…

I really want you
Really do
Really need you, baby
Really do
Well, I'm not real enough without you
Oh, what can I do?

You make me real
Only you, baby, have that appeal
So let me slide into your tender sunken sea
Make me free, love, make me free
Oh, yeah, babe

Well, roll now, baby, roll
You gotta roll now, baby, roll
Roll now, honey, roll
You gotta roll now, baby, roll

You make me real – *all right!*
You make me feel like lovers feel
You make me throw away mistake and misery
Make me free, love, make me free
Make me free
You make me – free, *yeah…*

Peace Frog   (Jim Morrison)

There's blood in the streets, it's up to my ankles
Blood in the streets, it's up to my knee   She came
Blood in the streets of the town of Chicago   She came
Blood on the rise, it's following me   She came

                                    just about the break of day
                              She came and then she drove away
                                          Sunlight in her hair

Blood in the streets runs a river of sadness, *yeah*   She came
Blood in the streets, it's up to my thigh   She came
Yeah, the river runs red down the legs of the city   She came
The women are crying red rivers of weeping   She came

                         She came in town and then she drove away
                                       Sunlight in her hair

                       Indians scattered on dawn's highway bleeding
                 Ghosts crowd the young child's fragile eggshell mind

Blood in the streets in the town of New Haven
Blood stains the roofs and the palm trees of Venice
Blood in my love in the terrible summer
Bloody red sun of phantastic L.A.

Blood! screams her brain as they chop off her fingers
Blood will be born in the birth of a nation
Blood is the rose of mysterious union

There's blood in the streets, it's up to my ankles
Blood in the streets, it's up to my knee
Blood in the streets of the town of Chicago
Blood on the rise, it's following me

Blue Sunday   (Jim Morrison)

I found my own true love was
on a blue Sunday
She looked at me and told me
I was the only
one in the world
Now I have found my girl

My girl awaits for me
in tender time
My girl is mine
She is the world
She is my girl

My girl awaits for me
in tender time
My girl is mine
She is the world
She is my girl

Ship Of Fools   (Jim Morrison)

The human race was dying out
No one left to scream and shout
People walking on the moon
Smog will get you pretty soon

Everyone was hanging out
Hanging up and hanging down
Hanging in and holding fast
Hope our little world will last

Yeah, along came Mister Goodtrips
Looking for a new ship
Ah, come on, people, better climb on board
Ah, come on, baby, now – going home

Ship of fools
Ship of fools

The human race was dying out
No one left to scream and shout
People walking on the moon
Smog gonna get you pretty soon

Ship of fools, ship of fools
Ship of fools, ship of fools

Ship of fools
Ship of fools
Ship of fools

Yeah, climb on board now
The ship's gonna leave you all far behind
I gotta climb on board, *yeah*

Ship of fools
Ship of fools
Ship of fools

Land Ho!   (Jim Morrison)

Grandma loved a sailor
who sailed the frozen sea
Grandpa was that whaler
and he took me on his knee
He said, "Son, I'm going crazy
from living on the land.
Got to find my shipmates
and walk on foreign sands."
Yeah

This old man was graceful
with silver in his smile
He smoked a briar pipe and
he walked four country miles
Singing songs of shady sisters
and old time liberty
Songs of love and songs of death
Songs to set men free
Hey!

I've got three ships and sixty men
A course for ports unread
I'll stand at mast, let north winds blow
Till half of us are dead

Land Ho!!

Well, if I get my hands on a dollar bill
Gonna buy a bottle and drink my fill
If I get my hands on a number five
Gonna skin that little girl alive
If I get my hands on a number two
Come back home and
marry you
marry you
marry you
All right

Hey – Land Ho!
Hey – Land Ho!

Well, if I get back home and I feel alright
You know, babe, I'm gonna love you tonight
Love tonight, *yeah*
Love tonight, *yeah*

Hey – Land Ho!
Hey – Land Ho!
Hey – Land Ho!

The Spy   (Jim Morrison)

I'm a spy in the house of love
I know the dream that you're dreaming of
I know the word that you long to hear
I know your deepest secret fear

I'm a spy in the house of love
I know the dream that you're dreaming of
I know the word that you long to hear
I know your deepest secret fear

I know everything
Everything you do
Everywhere you go
Everyone you know

I'm a spy in the house of love
I know the dream that you're dreaming of
I know the word that you long to hear
I know your deepest secret fear
I know your deepest secret fear
I know your deepest secret fear

I'm a spy
I can see you
What you do
And I know

Queen Of The Highway   (Jim Morrison)

She was a princess, queen of the highway
Sign on the road said, "Take us to Madre"
No one could save her, save the blind tiger
He was a monster, black dressed in leather
She was a princess, queen of the highway

Now they are wedded, she is a good girl
Naked as children, out in the meadow
Naked as children, wild as can be
Soon to have off-spring
Start it all over
Start it all over – *yeah*

American boy, American girl
Most beautiful people in the world
Son of a frontier Indian swirl
Dance into the midnight whirlpool
Formless

Hope it can continue a little while longer
Come on

Indian Summer   (Jim Morrison)

I love you the best
Better than all the rest
I love you the best
Better than all the rest
That I meet in the summer
Indian Summer

That I meet in the summer
Indian Summer

I love you the best
Better than all the rest

Maggie M'Gill   (Jim Morrison)

Miss Maggie M'Gill, she lived on a hill
Her daddy got drunk and left her no will
So she went down
Down to Tangie Town
People down there really like to get it on

Now, if you're sad and you're feeling blue
Go out and buy a brand new pair of shoes
And you go down
Down to Tangie Town
'Cause people down there really like to get it on
Get it on – *yeah*

Illegitimate son of a rock 'n' roll star
Illegitimate son of a rock 'n' roll star
Mom met Dad in the back of a rock 'n' roll car
Yeah

Well, I'm an old blues man
And I think that you understand
I've been singing the blues ever since the world began
Yeah

Maggie, Maggie, Maggie M'Gill
Roll on, roll on, Maggie M'Gill

Maggie, Maggie, Maggie M'Gill
Roll on, roll on, Maggie M'Gill

Maggie, Maggie, Maggie M'Gill
Roll on, roll on, Maggie M'Gill

Maggie, Maggie
Roll on, roll
Roll on, Maggie M'Gill
Roll on, roll

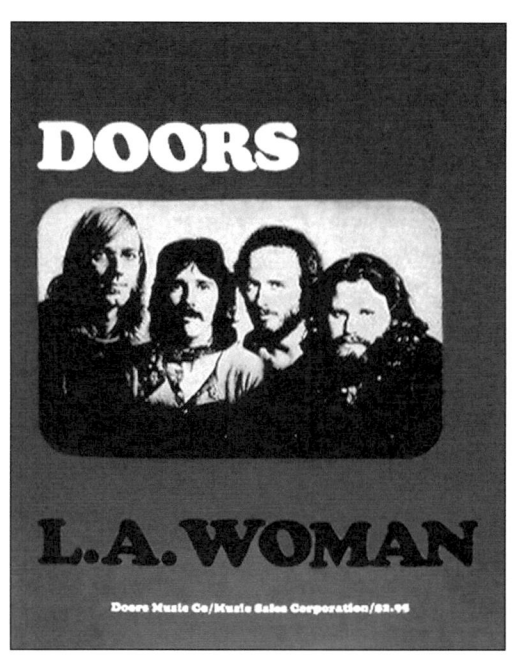

Los Angeles Free Press, USA, 30 April 1971
L.A. Woman

The Doors, sometimes known as Jim Morrison and Company, are no more. The rumor has been circulating for some time, and it was finally confirmed to me last week. Jim Morrison was the first to split, supposedly to further his film work and continue writing. The three remaining members, Robby Krieger, Ray Manzarek and John Densmore, have left Elektra Records and are planning on putting together some kind of a group of their own.

It is unfortunate that the last Doors album should amount to little more than just 'another album by The Doors'. Jim Morrison's pseudo-poetic lyric images have really worn a bit thin, and his literary borrowings (*Ship Of Fools, Land Ho!* and now *Been Down So Long*) show clearly that his originality is limited. His overly forceful, almost recitative vocal style is also very hard to take. There is at least one cut, *Hyacinth House*, which proves that he can actually sing when he wants to, and there is a brief but brilliant vocal imitation of a guitar on *Cars Hiss By My Window*. Perhaps it is only laziness, but Morrison has certainly never lived up to the potential (both as a singer and writer) of the very first Doors album. Jim is certainly in the twilight of his career.

On the plus side, we have the music, and a great plus that is. I had the distinct pleasure of listening to the first test pressing of L.A. WOMAN with Ray Manzarek, Robby Krieger and John Densmore, and I learned some interesting things about the album. It was recorded in The Doors' rehearsal hall and most of the cuts were done totally live – including the vocals.

This is the first Doors album where I have been really conscious of the music and the musicians. And musically, The Doors have to be one of the tightest and most inventive groups playing today. Robby Krieger is without question one of the best, most tasteful guitar players working, and Ray Manzarek's keyboard style seems to be so sure as to even have a sense of humor (check out the organ riff in the middle of *Hyacinth House*). I would not be at all surprised if their new group turned out to be something to watch.

So this is it: the last Doors album. There are a couple of cuts that stand out as a notch or two above the rest. *L'America*, written originally for *Zabriskie Point* but ultimately rejected by Antonioni, is a fine musical achievement, and *Riders On The Storm* is the group's most successfully ambitious piece in some time and is almost good enough to have been included on the first album.

L.A. WOMAN is not a bad album, it's just not a very good one, considering the potential of the talent involved.

?, GB, 17 July 1971
Stale and sterile Mister Morrison

L.A. WOMAN stands as their nadir, a spunkless, sterile effort that sounds as if this album has been put out just so that everyone won't forget the name, and of course, the name is Jim Morrison. He sounds deadly tired and mechanical; it becomes even more obvious here how monotonous is his voice, how it never rises above one level of intonation. He's still got the aspirations – he does Hooker's *Crawling King Snake* (very poorly) and a number called *The Changeling* – but no longer the conviction. The rest of the album – with the exception of *Riders On The Storm*, which has some effective electric piano (Ray Manzarek has always kept things very simple while establishing the basic texture of the music) – has the same staleness. *Cars Hiss By My Window* is a blatant nick, right down to the drumming style, of Jimmy Reed's *Baby, What's On Your Mind*, and includes some awful caterwauling from Morrison right at the end. *L.A. Woman*, the title song, sounds half the time like *Johnny B. Goode*. It's all so obvious that originality has left them.

Rolling Stone, USA, 27 May 1971
L.A. Woman

The Doors have never been more together. It's the first time since *The End* and *When The Music's Over* that they've been able to pull off anything interesting in the way of long cuts. And there are two of them here, *L.A. Woman* and *Riders On The Storm*, both of them minor monsters. And I'll be a monkey's uncle if *The WASP (Texas Radio & The Big Beat)* doesn't showcase Morrison's finest command of spoken jive to date, far superior to *Horse Latitudes*, and a demonstration of lyric-supporting timing. You can kick me in the ass for saying this (I don't mind): This is The Doors' greatest album (including their first) and the best album so far this year. A landmark worthy of dancing in the streets.

New Musical Express, GB, 16 July 1971
Controversial Doors

The Doors' music has always been a topic for controversy and this, their new and what could also be their last album has been greeted with mixed reviews and divided opinions.

You either like The Doors or you don't – it's as simple as that. Personally, I find L.A. WOMAN to be one of their best in quite some time. Accusations of it being insipid, tired and monotonous are, I feel, for the most part unfounded, for many cuts on this album have great depth, vigor and presence.

I think their overall relaxation has been misconstrued for lethargy and the fact that Jimbo and friends are playing in very basic rock and blues styles is alien to the preconceived opinions which many people may have about this band.

The inclusion of bassist Jerry Scheff really fills out the sound and makes Ray Manzarek (keyboards), Robby Krieger (guitar) and John Densmore (drums) get-it-on in true rockin' fashion. In fact, on half the tracks the group sound really happy and enthusiastic with what they are laying down. *The Changeling* and the title track, *L.A. Woman*, are up-tempo rockers with Jim really roaring out the lyrics. *Love Her Madly* has a typical syncopated early Doors sound about it with a Mrs. Mills piano line from Manzarek. *L'America*, *Hyacinth House* and *Riders On The Storm* (complete with rainstorm effects) are true Doors originals. In contrast, their interpretation of John Lee Hooker's *Crawling King Snake* is less effective, as is *Cars Hiss By My Window*.

Perhaps the two outstanding, if somewhat untypical, Doors cuts are *Been Down So Long* and *The WASP (Texas Radio & The Big Beat)*. The former is very R&B'ish and reminiscent of Albert King's *The Hunter*, a cut which has Morrison really roaring the vocal out as the rhythm section lay down a rock solid back beat. *The WASP* is a classic of its kind, for while Scheff and Densmore do their darndest to blow your stereo speakers Morrison recites his prose before the entire band explodes into the melody line.

Before Morrison's untimely passing, both he and The Doors had parted company. If this is to be their final statement, it is a good one and should be given a few hearings before passing judgement.

The Changeling   (Jim Morrison)

Ooh! Do it!
Do-do!

I live uptown
I live downtown
I live all around

I had money
I had none
I had money
I had none
But I never been so broke
that I couldn't leave town

I'm a changeling
See me change
I'm a changeling
See me change

I'm the air you breathe
Food you eat
Friends you greet
In the swarming street
Wow!

See me change
See me change

Get loose!

I live uptown
I live downtown
I live all around

I had money – *yeah!*
I had none
I had money – *yeah!*
And I had none
But I never been so broke
that I couldn't leave town – *babe*

Well, I'm the air you breathe
Food you eat
Friends you greet
In the swarming street
Wow!

Uh! You better... Ooh! Uh!
You gotta see me change
See me change

Yeah, I'm leaving town
On the midnight train
Gonna see me change

Change, change, change
Change, change, change
Change, change, change
Change, change, change

Well, change
Change
Change

Love Her Madly   (Robby Krieger)

Don't you love her madly
Don't you need her badly
Don't you love her ways
Tell me what you say
Don't you love her madly
Wanna be her daddy
Don't you love her face

Don't you love her as she's walking out the door
Like she did one thousand times before
Don't you love her ways
Tell me what you say
Don't you love her as she's walking out the door

All your love
All your love
All your love
All your love
All your love is gone
So sing a lonely song
Of a deep blue dream
Seven horses seem
To be on the mark

Yeah – don't you love her
Don't you love her as she's walking out the door

All your love
All your love
All your love
Yeah...
All your love is gone
So sing a lonely song
Of a deep blue dream
Seven horses seem
To be on the mark

Well, don't you love her madly
Ah, don't you love her madly
Yeah, don't you love her madly

Been Down So Long   (Jim Morrison)

Well, I've been down so goddamn long
That it looks like up to me
Well, I've been down so very damn long
That it looks like up to me
Yeah, why don't one you people
Come on and set me free

I said, warden, warden, warden
Won't you break your lock and key
I said, warden, warden, warden
Won't you break your lock and key
Yeah, come along here, mister
Come on and let the poor boy be

Baby, baby, baby
Won't you get down on your knee
Baby, baby, baby
Oh won't you get down on your knees
Come on, little darling, *yeah*
Come on and give your love to me
Oh yeah

Well, I've been down so goddamn long
Well, it looks like up to me
Well, I've been down so very damn long
Yeah, it looks like up to me
Yeah, why don't some you people
Come on
Come on
Come on
and set me free!

Cars Hiss By My Window   (Jim Morrison)

The cars hiss by my window
Like the waves down on the beach
The cars hiss by my window
Like the waves down on the beach
I got this girl beside me
But she's out of reach

Headlight through my window
Shining on the wall
Headlight through my window
Shining on the wall
Can't hear my baby
Though I call and call

Windows start *a*-trembling
With a sonic boom
Windows start *a*-trembling
With a sonic boom – boom
A cold girl'll *a*-kill you
In a darkened room

Right!
Right on!

L.A. Woman   (Jim Morrison)

Well, I just got into town about an hour ago
Took a look around, see which way the wind blow
Where the little girls in their Hollywood bungalows

Are you a lucky little lady in the City of Light?
Or just another lost angel –
City of Night
City of Night
City of Night
City of Night
Wow!
Come on!

L.A. Woman
L.A. Woman
L.A. Woman Sunday afternoon
L.A. Woman Sunday afternoon
L.A. Woman Sunday afternoon
Drive through your suburbs
Into your blues
Into your blues – *yeah!*
Into your blue-blue Blues
Into your blues
Oh... yeah!

I see your hair is burning
Hills are filled with fire
If they say I never loved you
You know they are a liar
Driving down your freeways
Midnight alleys roam
Cops in cars, the topless bars
Never saw a woman –
So alone
So alone, *yeah*
So alone
So alone

Motel Money Murder Madness
Let's change the mood from glad to sadness

Mr. Mojo Risin'
Mr. Mojo Risin'
Mr. Mojo Risin'
Mr. Mojo Risin'
Got to keep on rising
Mr. Mojo Risin'
Mr. Mojo Risin'
Mojo rising
Got my mojo rising
Mr. Mojo Risin'
You got to keep on rising
Rising, rising
Going right in, right in
I'm gonna ride in, right in
I've gotta ride in, right in
Well, right in, right in
I gotta...
Wow! Yeah! Right! Come on!
Yeah...

Well, just got into town about an hour ago
Took a look around, see which way the wind blow
Where the little girls in their Hollywood bungalows

Are you a lucky little lady in the City of Light?
Or just another lost angel –
City of Night
City of Night
City of Night
City of Night
Wow!
Come on!

L.A. Woman
L.A. Woman
L.A. Woman
You're my woman
My little L.A. Woman
Yeah, my L.A. Woman
Hey, hey, woman, come on
L.A. Woman, come on

L'America   (Jim Morrison)

Yeah…

I took a trip down to Lamerica
To trade some beads for a pint of gold
I took a trip down to Lamerica
To trade some beads for a pint of gold

Lamerica, Lamerica, Lamerica
Lamerica, Lamerica, Lamerica

Come on, people, don't you look so down
You know the Rain-Man's coming to town
He'll change your weather, change your luck
And then he'll teach you how to
Find your Self

Lamerica

Friendly strangers came to town
All the people put them down
But the women loved their ways
Ah, come again some other day
Like the gentle rain
Like the gentle rain that falls

I took a trip down to Lamerica
To trade some beads for a pint of gold
I took a trip down to Lamerica
To trade some beads for a pint of gold

Lamerica, Lamerica, Lamerica
Lamerica, Lamerica, Lamerica

Lamerica

Hyacinth House   (Jim Morrison)

What are they doing in the Hyacinth House
What are they doing in the Hyacinth House
To please the lions – *yeah* – this day?

I need a brand new friend who doesn't bother me
I need a brand new friend who doesn't trouble me
I need someone – *yeah* – who doesn't need me

I see the bathroom is clear
I think that somebody's near
I'm sure that someone is following me
Oh yeah

Why did you throw the Jack of Hearts away?
Why did you throw the Jack of Hearts away?
It was the only card in the deck that I had left to play

And I'll say it again, I need a brand new friend
And I'll say it again, I need a brand new friend
And I'll say it again, I need a brand new friend – the end

Crawling King Snake   (John Lee Hooker / Arr.: Jim Morrison)

Well, I'm the crawling king snake
and I rule my den
I'm the crawling king snake
and I rule my den
Yeah, don't mess 'round with my mate,
gonna use her for myself

Caught me crawling, baby
when the grass was very high
I keep on crawling
till the day I die
Crawling king snake
and I rule my den
You better give me what I want,
gonna crawl no more

Caught me crawling, baby,
crawling 'round your door
See anything I want,
I'm gonna crawl on your floor
Let's crawl
And I rule my den
Come on, give me what I want,
ain't gonna crawl no more
Ah, let's crawl a while

Come on, crawl
Come on, crawl
Get on out there on your
hands and knees, baby
Crawl all over me
Just like the spider on the wall,
ooh – we gone crawl
One more!

Well, I'm the crawling king snake
and I rule my den
Call me the crawling king snake
and I rule my den
Yeah, don't mess 'round with my mate,
gonna use her for myself

The WASP
(Texas Radio & The Big Beat)   (Jim Morrison)

I wanna tell you about
Texas Radio & The Big Beat

It comes out of the Virginia Swamps,
cool and slow,
with plenty of precision
and a back beat
narrow and hard to master

Some call it heavenly
in its brilliance
Others, mean and rueful
of the Western Dream

I love the friends I have
gathered together on this thin raft
We have constructed Pyramids
in honor of our escaping
This is the land where
the Pharaoh died

The Negroes in the forest,
brightly feathered,
and they are saying:
«Forget the Night.
Live with us in forests
of azure. Out here
on the perimeter there
are no stars; out
here we is stoned –
immaculate.»

Now listen to this,
I tell you about the Heartache
I tell you about the
Heartache and the loss of God
I tell you about the hopeless night,
the meager food for souls forgot
I tell you about the maiden
with wrought-iron soul

I tell you this:
No eternal reward will forgive us now
for wasting the dawn

I tell you about
Texas Radio & The Big Beat
Soft-driven slow and mad
like some new language

Now listen to this,
I tell you about Texas
I tell you about Texas – Radio
I tell you about the hopeless night,
the wandering, the Western Dream
Tell you about the maiden
with wrought-iron soul

Riders On The Storm   (Jim Morrison)

Riders on the storm
Riders on the storm
Into this house we're born
Into this world we're thrown
Like a dog without a bone
An actor out on loan
Riders on the storm

There's a killer on the road
His brain is squirming like a toad
Take a long holiday
Let your children play
If you give this man a ride
Sweet family will die
Killer on the road
Yeah...

Girl you gotta love your man
Girl you gotta love your man
Take him by the hand
Make him understand
The world on you depends
Our life will never end
Gotta love your man
Yeah...

Riders on the storm
Riders on the storm
Into this house we're born
Into this world we're thrown
Like a dog without a bone
An actor out on loan
Riders on the storm

Riders on the storm
Riders on the storm
Riders on the storm
Riders on the storm

J.M. / Doors

L.A. Woman

Well, I just got into town about
an hour ago

Took a look around, see which
way the wind blow

Where the little girls in their
Hollywood Bungalows

Are you a lucky little lady in
The City of Light?

Or just another lost angel
City of Night (?)

L.A. Woman (x) (2)

L.A. Woman Sunday afternoon (3)

Drive thru your suburbs

into your blues (x) (2)

into your blue-blue Blues

into your blues

J.M. / Doors

L.A. Woman

Well, I just got into town about
an hour ago

Took a look around, see which
way the wind blow

Where the little girls in their
Hollywood Bungalows

Are you a lucky little lady in
The City of Light?

Or just another lost angel
City of Night

L.A. Woman (2)

L.A. Woman Sunday afternoon (3)
— Drive thru your suburbs (2)

into your blues (2)

into your blue-blue Blue

into your blues

Break
I see your hair is burning
Hills are fill'd w/ fire

If They say I never loved you
You know They are a liar

Drivin' down your Freeways
Midnite alley's roam

Cops in cars, The topless bars
Never saw a woman —

So alone (2)
So alone-lone Lone
So alone

Motel money murder Madness

Let's change The mood from glad
To Sadness

I see your hair is burning
Hills are filled w/fire

If They say I never loved you
You know they are a liar

Midnight alley's, roam
Cops in cars, The topless bars
Never saw a woman so alone
So alone, so alone, so alone

Motel money, murder Madness
Lets change The mood
from glad To Sadness

Mister mojo risin' (4)
Got To keep on risin'
Mister mojo risin' (2)
mojo risin'

Break
Mr. Mojo Risin' (4)
Keep on risin'
Got t. keep on risin'
Risin' risin' (8)

Repeat 1st Verse
down to... "City of Night"

L.A. Woman (2)
She's my woman
Little L.A. Woman
L.A. Woman C'mon

Got to keep on risin'
Risin', risin'
Goin' right on right in (2)
right on right in

Well, I just got into town about
an hour ago
Took a look around, see which
way the wind blow
Where the little girls in their
Hollywood bungalows
Are you a lucky little lady in
The City of Light?
Or just another lost angel
City of Night (1)

L.A. Woman (✻) (3)
you're my woman
A✻ little L.A.Woman L.A. Woman
Hey, Hey come-on
L.A. Woman come-on

J.L. Hooker — arr. by Doors

Crawling King Snake

I'm the crawling king snake
& I rule my den (2)
Don't mess round w/ my mate
gonna use her for myself

Caught me crawlin' baby
when the grass was very high
Keep on crawlin' til the
day I die

I'm a crawlin' king snake
& I rule my den

Gimme what I want I want no more
aint gonna crawl no more

Caught me crawlin' baby
crawlin' round your door
See anything I want, I'm
gonna crawl on your floor

C'mon, crawl (2)
Get on out there on your hands & knees baby
Crawl all over me
Just like the spider on the wall
we gone crawl

J.M. / Doors

L'america

I took a trip down to
L'america
To trade some beads for
a pint of gold (2)

L'america (3) (3)

C'mon people don't you look
so down
you know the rainman's
coming to town

He'll change your weather
He'll change your luck

He'll even teach you, how to
Find yourself

L'america (3) (3)

Friendly strangers came to town
All the people put them down
But the women loved their ways
Come again some other day

Like the gentle rain that falls
Like the gentle rain that falls

Repeat verse 1

Verse 2
The Negroes in the forest,
brightly feathered,
& they are saying:
« Forget the Night.
Live w/ us in forests
of azure. Out here
on the perimeter there
are no stars; out
here we is stoned —
immaculate. »

Break:

Let me tell you about Texas
Let me tell you about Texas —
Radio.

Tell you about the wandering,
The hopeless night,
The Western Dream
Tell you about the maiden w/ soul
wrought-iron soul

JIM/DOORS

The Wasp

I want to tell you about
Texas Radio
&
The Big Beat

It comes out of the Virginia
Swamps, cool & slow
w/ a back beat narrow
& hard to master

Some call it heavenly
in its brilliance

Others, mean & ruful
of the Western Dream

I love the friends I have
gathered together on this
Thin raft

We have invented Pyramids
in honor of our escaping
This is the land where
The Pharaoh died
Break

JIM / DOORS

Riders On The Storm

Riders on the storm (2)
Into this house we're born
Into this world we're thrown
Like a dog without a bone
An actor out on loan
Riders on the storm

There's a killer on the road
His brain is squirming like a toad
Take a long holiday
Let your children play
If you give this man a ride
Sweet family will die
There's a killer on the road

Girl you gotta love your man (2)
Take him by the hand
Make him understand
The world on you depends
Our life will never end
Girl you gotta love your man

(Repeat)   .

Riders on the storm (9)

I want to Tell you about
Texas Radio & The Big Beat
Soft-driven slow & mad
like some new language

Instrumental

Let me Tell you about
Heartache

Let me Tell you about
Heartache & The loss of God

Tell you about The wandering
The hopeless night, The
Western Dream

Tell you about The maiden
w/ wrought-iron soul.

Interview with Jim Morrison
ZigZag, GB, October 1970

Whilst at the Isle of Wight festival, John managed to interview Jim Morrison:

Z: I've discovered a book on sale at this festival called "The Doors Song Book", which appears to be a pirated version of all the words off all the albums, including the new one. What do you reckon about that?

J: Well, I don't mind if they've got all the words spelt right. A lot of the time they really screw up the meaning, just one word or one semi colon can ruin the whole thing.

Z: Do you approve of having the lyrics on the back of your album or on the inside sleeve, because in England, two of them have had the lyrics and three haven't. Do you think it makes a difference? We didn't have the words to 'The Unknown Soldier' for instance.

J: Yeah, they really got botched up. I don't think it matters. I don't think it's necessary but ...

Z: You don't mind that somebody's making some bread out of your words?

J: No, what harm could it do?

Note: This interview by John Tobler is the only existing interview where Jim Morrison talks about printed versions of his lyrics.

Index of Songs

Illustrations

11, 31, 32, 39, 50, 89, 107, 116–121: Handwritten lyrics by Jim Morrison.

13 Music Sheet *Light My Fire*, USA, August 1968. Foto: November 1966.

17 Music Sheet *Light My Fire*, USA, October 1969. Fotos: September 1967.

19 Music Sheet *Light My Fire*, USA, 1970. Foto: September 1967.

26 EP *Light My Fire*, France, 1967 / Single *Love Me Two Times*, France, 1967
Single *Love Me Two Times*, Italy, 1967 / Single *Roadhouse Blues*, Italy, 1970.

27 Music Sheet *People Are Strange*, USA, October 1967. Foto: September 1967.

28 Single *Tell All The People*, Sweden, 1969. Foto: November 1966.

40, 41, 42: Reprint of the inner sleeve of the original LP STRANGE DAYS.

52 Music Sheet *Hello, I Love You*, USA, July 1968. Foto: March 1968.

54 Single *The Unknown Soldier*, Italy, April 1968. Foto: September 1967.

55 Elektra Records promotional poster, USA, March 1968.

67 Music Sheet *Touch Me*, USA, December 1968. Foto: November 1966.

73 Single *Wishful Sinful*, Holland, May 1969. Foto: Elektra advertisement, 1969.

82, 83, 84: Reprint of the inner sleeve of the original LP THE SOFT PARADE.

85 Elektra Records advertisement for MORRISON HOTEL, USA, March 1970.

93 Single *Love Her Madly*, Sweden, 1971. Foto: January 1970.

99 Songbook *L.A. Woman*, USA, May 1971
Elektra Records promotional poster for L.A. WOMAN, USA, April 1971.

102 Elektra Records promotional photo, March 1971.

104 Drawing by Thomas Collmer, 1986.

111 Elektra Records promotional photo, March 1971.

114 Music Sheet *Riders On The Storm*, USA, July 1971. Foto: March 1971.